T
Love,
JIM

THOUGHTS FOR REFLECTION

Thoughts for
Reflection

By
Rev. Albert J. Nimeth, O.F.M.

ST. PAUL EDITIONS

IMPRIMI POTEST:
  Germain Schwab, O.F.M.
  Minister Provincial

NIHIL OBSTAT:
  Marion A. Habig, O.F.M.
  Censor Deputatus

IMPRIMATUR:
  Rt. Rev. Msgr. Francis W. Byrne
  Vicar General, Archdiocese of Chicago

Library of Congress Catalog Card Number: 67-31354
(under title of first edition: *SUDDEN THOUGHTS*, © Franciscan Herald Press, 1967)

ISBN 0-8198-7331-4 c
     0-8198-7332-2 p

Printed in the U.S.A., by the Daughters of St. Paul
50 St. Paul's Ave., Boston, MA 02130

The Daughters of St. Paul are an international congregation of women religious serving the Church with the communications media.

Contents

1. Hasten To Help 13
2. Mirrored Goodness 14
3. Outer Limits 16
4. A Big Heart 17
5. Bond of Union 18
6. Ideal Exercises 20
7. Do You Care? 21
8. Pay the Price 23
9. Help at Hand 24
10. Appreciate Oneself 25
11. My Brother's Keeper 27
12. Dynamic Christian 28
13. Reassurance of God 29
14. Bread of Life 31
15. Secret Samaritans 32
16. Public Relations 34
17. Cool It 35
18. Living Word 36
19. Light and Love 38
20. Stepping Stones 39
21. Don't Be Hamstrung 40
22. Let There Be Light 41
23. Service Station 43
24. Wide Awake 44
25. Let in the Light 46
26. God's Helper 47
27. Don't Be a Robot 48
28. The Beauty of Sanctity . . 50
29. Stick With It 51
30. Be Careful 52
31. Measure of Love 54
32. Emmanuel 55
33. Unique Dignity 56
34. The Front Line 58
35. Our Way of Life 59

36. Grace of Working 61
37. A Dose of Prayer 62
38. Stay Fit 63
39. Crisis in Change 64
40. Source of Grace 66
41. Essence of Life 67
42. Now 68
43. St. Francis 70
44. Live Coals 71
45. 'Tis the Season 73
46. A Layman's Need 74
47. Beacon Light 75
48. Sure-Fire Formula 76
49. Goodness Gracious 77
50. Up-to-Date 79
51. The Lowest Height 80
52. Help Wanted 82
53. A Second Look 83
54. No Small Matter 84
55. Heart and Soul 85
56. Love-In 87
57. Christify Oneself 88
58. Love of Country 89
59. Uphill Battle 91
60. Capacity Load 92
61. Splinters 93
62. The Game of Life 95
63. Ordained Men 96
64. God Loves Me 97
65. Start Counting 98
66. Life and Love 100
67. Crown of Victory 101
68. Just One Moment 103
69. He Provides 104
70. Flaming Youth 105

71. Give Me Room........ 107
72. Contagious............ 108
73. Dear-Drops 109
74. Who Are You? 111
75. Grace's Foundation 112
76. God Is Love 114
77. Hub of Life........... 115
78. Small Beginnings 116
79. As You Travel Ask Us .. 118
80. Fount of Wisdom...... 119
81. Hidden Helps......... 120
82. Get With It........... 121
83. Weak or Meek 122
84. Stay With It 124
85. A Stormy Affair 125
86. Trustworthy........... 126
87. In God We Trust 128
88. To Each His Own 129
89. Super Power.......... 130
90. Our Mission 132
91. Work and Pray 133
92. Daily Invitation........ 134
93. 16670 136
94. Yours for the Asking ... 137
95. Think A-head 138
96. Deny Yourself......... 140
97. The Morning Offering.. 141
98. Fatherly Care 143
99. You Paint the Picture .. 144

100. The Good Book 146
101. Path of Sorrow 147
102. Who Cares?.......... 149
103. Basic Unit 150
104. The Will that Counts . 151
105. I Love You 152
106. Keep in Touch 154
107. Standards of Value 155
108. Delicate Balance...... 157
109. Mystery of the Cross . 158
110. Louis Pasteur 160
111. Friendship 161
112. Get the Facts 163
113. Creeping Cancer 164
114. The Solid Rock....... 165
115. Live It Up........... 167
116. Step Lightly 168
117. Literary Diet......... 170
118. Be Merciful.......... 171
119. Set Values 172
120. Lost and Found 174
121. He Ain't Heavy 175
122. Life's Poison 176
123. Heart-to-Heart 178
124. True Wisdom......... 179
125. Money's Not
Everything........... 181
126. Secrets of Youth 182
127. Long and Short of It.. 184
128. Do It Now........... 185

INTRODUCTION

Rev. John A. O'Brien

We are living in an age geared to speed. Journeys which took our forefathers in their covered wagons months to complete, we now make in jet planes in an hour or two. The demands of modern life necessitate us completing our varied tasks with ever-increasing speed.

This is true particularly in the field of reading. There has been an explosion of books in our country. If one is to get even the gist of the more worthwhile ones, he can do so only by reading digests of them. This explains the unprecedented popularity of *The Reader's Digest*.

Taking his cues from these conditions of modern life, Father Albert J. Nimeth, O.F.M., has written a book which gets its points across with unusual dispatch. Consisting of 128 short stories, incidents, anecdotes, sermonettes, reflections and meditations, *Thoughts for Reflection* is admirably suited to the busy people of today. The concrete character and vivid imagery of each of its reflections grips the reader's attention and holds him enthralled.

Covering a wide range of topics such as prayer, love, mercy, self-knowledge, habit, work, spiritual training, Sacred Scripture and a multitude of other timely topics, the book ministers to the tastes and needs of all thoughtful people today. Timely, well reasoned, written in a clear, crisp style, geared to the needs of our day, *Thoughts for Reflection* is a little masterpiece that merits millions of readers.

1 HASTEN TO HELP

James Davis, a construction worker, was doing his job thirty floors up. Suddenly, he heard somebody scream. In construction work when somebody screams that means only one thing — trouble. The shouts of anguish came from a man who was barely hanging on to the edge of the disposal chute. If he released his grip, he would surely plunge to his death thirty floors below. Without a second thought Davis was at his side. Only then did he realize it was his own son. Quick action and strong arms saved the man's life. After he had pulled his son to safety, Davis felt the impact of the incident. "Imagine," he said, "you start running to help somebody and suddenly you see it's your own son. Imagine how you would feel if you did not make it in time!"

Bonds of blood spur extra effort when someone is in trouble. When we recognize the person in need as someone near and dear to us, we do not count the cost and sacrifice in coming to his aid. What may start out as just another job involving just another person suddenly becomes a special job involving a special person.

It happens every day. Sometimes we recognize the special person. But in most cases we do not recognize the special person so we go about the task in a disinterested, desultory manner as if we were bored with the whole matter.

Can you imagine our wide-eyed and open-mouth surprise when we hear those strangely familiar words: "Come, blessed of my Father, take possession of the kingdom prepared for you from the foundation of the world; for I was hungry and you gave me to eat; I was thirsty and you gave me to drink; I was a stranger and you took me in; naked and you covered me; sick and you visited me; in prison and you came to me. Then the just will answer saying, "Lord, when did we see you hungry and feed you; thirsty and give you drink? And when did we see you a stranger and take you in, or naked and clothe you? Or when did we see you sick, or in prison and come to you?" And answering the king will say to them, "Amen, I say to you, as long as you did it for one of these, the least of my brethren, you did it to me."

When you think about it, everyone is special. Someone in need? Someone in trouble? Let's hasten to help. It may be a son. It may be a brother. It may be Christ. "Imagine how you would feel if you did not make it in time!"

> *Anyone who welcomes you welcomes me; and those who welcome me welcome the one who sent me* (MT. 10, 40).

2 MIRRORED GOODNESS

We had never met before, but when I greeted him he stopped dead in his tracks and gave me the oddest stare. In a sarcastic voice he said, "I don't know you and I don't care to know you. And I don't care to know anything with which you are associated." As he walked away in a huff, he shouted over his shoulder, "I lived without God all my life and I will continue to live without him."

I couldn't help feeling sorry for the man. He must be very miserable if a simple well-intentioned greeting could evoke such a vitriolic explosion. His heart must rankle with bitterness and venom. How empty his life must be because he will never recognize the goodness of God all around him. He does not see the goodness of God in the symphony and pageantry of nature. In his frame of mind he will never experience the goodness of God in a truly good man. "A truly good man," says Peter Lippert, "is a walking prayer, a morning and evening hymn become flesh in the sight of his fellowman." His heart will never glow with gratitude and wonder, with admiration and love that the numerous manifestations of God's goodness ought to engender.

He does not know it, but that man himself is the object of God's pursuing love. He is searching, searching he knows not for what. He tries one substitute after the other only, in the end, to taste the emptiness of it all. The residue is bitter. Afraid lest in having God he can have "nought else besides," so he won't take his chances with God. Little does he realize that this is precisely the reason why he will have "nought else besides."

What meaning can a life possibly have that has no relationship with God? It has to be a dull existence, purposeless, aimless. When you meet someone like this, the words of St. Augustine seem more true than ever. "Our hearts are made for God and they are restless until they rest in him."

The more I thought about that man, the more I was troubled. I began to reproach myself for not being the type of person in whom the goodness could shine forth in such a way as to break through this wall of rejection. Perhaps he has been hardened because of exposure to too many pious frauds. Perhaps in his previous encounters he found Christians poor personal propaganda for the ideals they profess. Does the fault lie with too many of us who refuse to be effective instruments that God can use to draw people to himself?

> *You are the light of the world. No one lights a lamp to put it under a tub; they put it on a lampstand where it shines for everyone in the house. In the same way your light must shine in the sight of men so that, seeing your good works, they may give praise to your Father in heaven* (Mt. 5, 14-16).

3   OUTER LIMITS

Every time I take a plane ride, I can't help admiring the great progress man has made in harnessing the elements to work for him. Once the principles of aerodynamics were mastered, the sky was the limit literally. Look at what has happened in the short span of a little over sixty years since Kitty Hawk. Sputnik, agena rockets, telestar, gemini space project — an entirely new vocabulary has heralded the dawn of a new era. Regular trips into space, perhaps to the Moon, seem to be just around the corner. With the aid of science, man is pushing back the frontiers. Strange, isn't it, how man at one time thought he had reached the end of the line, like Alexander the Great looking for more nations to conquer. Then the breakthrough and a whole new vista opens before our very eyes. Man can be proud of his accomplishments.

There is, however, one danger we must avoid — the danger that man will think himself greater than he really is just because he has mastered a few laws and subjected the forces of nature. There is ever present the danger that man will succumb to the whispering of the wily serpent in the garden of progress: "You will become like God." Just as soon as we get "too big for our britches," we distort the true picture. To avoid a perversion of values, we must keep God in the proper relationship with the achievements of man.

Keep God in the picture, then the mind of man can soar to even greater heights without running the risk of creating a Frankenstein. With God in the picture we can marvel how vastly superior man is to any other form of visible creation. This straining for new fields to conquer demonstrates that the spirit of man cannot be shackled. That spirit can go on yearning for more and more. And it does. So great is its capacity that it can never be satisfied until it gets beyond creatures and reaches its fulfillment in God.

We feel that the new era opening before our eyes will hold many more wonders. As the vastness and beauty of the universe become more evident to man, he will have to go down on his knees in unbelievable amazement. Then we will have the experience of St. Francis all over again — man finding God in his creation, man using creatures as a stepping stone back to the Creator.

4 A BIG HEART

During the last war in Germany, a little girl was walking along a dusty road with her sisters. On all sides were the ravages of the war. The group stopped before a wayside shrine to say a prayer. When they came to the part in the Our Father — "forgive us our trespasses as . . .", they paused. Overhead in the distance they heard the angry roar of enemy planes. Startled and anxious, the children were uncertain about continuing. An army general had viewed the drama, unobserved. When he noticed the children's predicament, he completed the prayer in a loud voice, "as we forgive those who trespass against us." Battle-scarred and weary, he meant every word he said. This was but an echo of "Father, forgive them for they know not what they do."

One of the outstanding virtues preached and practiced by Christ was forgiveness. This he taught on many occasions. The parable of the prodigal son is a well-known instance. Another is the case of the woman taken in adultery. When the mob had turned against her, intent on stoning her as the law of Moses prescribed, Christ dared to stand up to adverse public opinion to teach forgiveness. If anyone had authority to condemn her, he had. Instead he says, "He that is without sin, let him cast the first stone." As the crowd thinned out, driven away by a guilty conscience, Christ stood alone with the woman. "Does no man condemn you?" "No one, Lord." "Then neither will I condemn you."

This incident may not strike us as spectacular, but it gives a hint to something more demanding. On the heights of Calvary, when all forces of evil clamored for his destruction, Christ finds an excuse for forgiveness. Divine wisdom who knows the heart of man prays, "Father, forgive them for they know not what they do."

We glibly repeat these words, but often we forget the intolerable anguish of body and soul in which those words were spoken. It was the most awful of death throes, the fiercest pangs of dereliction that were calmly put aside as he sought forgiveness for his enemies.

This is a hard lesson for us to learn, but learn it we must, if our heart is to be truly Christian. When we are wronged, let's not imagine that the offense is so monstrous as to be unpardonable. If Christ does not draw the line, why should we? It was St. Francis who said, "It is in pardoning that we are pardoned." Each in his own way must re-echo this echo of Christ.

> *Never have grudges against others, or lose your temper, or raise your voice to anybody, or call each other names, or allow any sort of spitefulness. Be friends with one another, and kind, forgiving each other readily as God forgave you in Christ* (EPH. 4, 31-32).

5 BOND OF UNION

The family that eats together, stays together." This is how Fr. John Thomas S.J. of St. Louis University paraphrases Fr. Peyton's famous statement: "The family that prays together stays together." I like the idea. Without minimizing the necessity of family prayer, it is important to stress the need that families take their meals as a family.

There is something special and sacred about a meal. Not everybody is invited to put his feet under our table and share our meals. This privilege is reserved for particular people whom we value for one reason or another.

Our Lord used the occasion of a meal to institute the Blessed Eucharist. He revealed himself to the disciples of Emmaus at a meal. The early Christians had their agape, love feast, to indicate their community of spirit. We often honor important persons at a banquet. The fringes and frills of banquets and meals may leave something to be desired, but we cannot escape the essential idea that sharing a meal is replete with meaning.

There is something sacred, therefore, about a family meal. The bond of union, the community of interest and aspiration can certainly be fostered effectively by regular family meals. Here the father assumes his rightful place as head of the family, a role too often forfeited. At a family meal the children experience their dependence on the father who has provided the means of sustaining life. Here the tender loving care of mother is served up with each dish she prepares. The family meal can be full of meaning; it can be an effective means of cementing family relations and establishing a sense of security so necessary in our frenetic world.

However, what is the situation in many a family today? Often meals are taken on the run because each member in the family has a separate schedule to meet. We no longer plan our day around the family meal. We plan it around our bowling league, our night school, our dates, our extra family activities. This is a topsy-turvy business. We are abetting the very forces that are tearing our families apart.

Why not call a moratorium on all these extras until once again the family meal is given the importance it deserves. By emphasizing this once-a-day get-together, perhaps we may be able to withstand the disintegrating influences that are working havoc with family living. We have to start somewhere. Why not here?

"The family that eats together stays together."

If you go snapping at each other and tearing each other to pieces, you had better watch or you will destroy the whole community (GAL. 5, 15).

6   IDEAL EXERCISES

A little knowledge is a dangerous thing. Especially if the knowledge is about ourselves. One reason why so few people make progress in developing their spiritual life is because they do not know themselves. So much of the knowledge that we have about ourselves is glossed over by an exaggerated opinion of ourselves. Most of us imagine we have greater talent and greater virtue than the facts warrant.

The lack of self-knowledge is due primarily to the dread of taking an honest look at ourselves and being brutally honest in appraising our true worth. If we knew ourselves as we truly are, we would avoid two pitfalls — overestimating ourselves, which leads to false superiority; and under-estimating ourselves, which leads to false inferiority. Somewhere in between we find our true selves.

A very important aid in discovering our true selves is the daily examination of conscience. If we take an unabashed look at ourselves, at least once a day, gradually the scales will fall from our eyes.

It takes courage to look at ourselves. Because so many of us lack this courage, we neglect this wholesome practice. It is so much more comfortable to remain in blissful ignorance. Nobody likes to have his circles disturbed. Self-knowledge will do just that. It will disturb our circles because it will reveal to us how much there is to be done before we attain the degree of perfection intended by God.

It is precisely in this that the value of self-knowledge lies. We cannot look at ourselves day after day, see how much work is to be done, and still remain complacent about it. One of two things will happen — either we will stop looking at ourselves because we can't stand the sight, or we will make the necessary changes in order to look at something more worthwhile.

The value of self-scrutiny cannot be denied. As the knowledge of self increases, a knowledge of our ideal becomes more clear. And there is no more effective spur than a clear knowledge of our ideal.

However, since the practice of self-examination goes against the grain, it is important that we nail ourselves down to a definite time in our daily schedule. Set aside five or ten minutes when you can get away from the hustle and bustle of daily demands. Close the door to the numerous distractions and sit down to think. Think about yourself; think about God. These few moments must be sacrosanct. Under no circumstances make any exception. This exercise ought to be as much a part of our daily life as taking food. In the beginning we will find countless excuses for making exceptions. The first exception will be the fatal one. Because if we skip one day, it will be easier to skip the next. Before long we will be right back where we started. But if we persevere, we will no longer be plagued by the danger of a little self-knowledge.

> *To listen to the word and not obey it is like looking at your own features in a mirror, and then, after a quick look, going off and immediately forgetting what you look like. But the man who looks steadily at the perfect law of freedom and makes that his habit — not listening and then forgetting, but actively putting it into practice — will be happy in all he does* (JAM. I, 23-25).

7   DO YOU CARE?

Pfc. Milton Lee Olive of Chicago was listed among the casualties of the Vietnam war. There was something different about his death just as there was something different about the young man himself. His is a spirit that is needed so badly in a selfish world in which man does not want to get involved with fellow man.

Milton Olive and four buddies huddled near a thicket at Oi An in a life and death struggle to escape the shrapnel from the Viet Cong grenades. Suddenly, someone shouted: "Look out. A grenade!" It landed in front of the group, bounced twice and came to rest at the feet of Olive. As his companions scrambled for cover, Olive without a moment's hesitation grabbed the grenade and tucked it under his stomach. Hunched over it he let it explode. He sacrificed his life for his fellow soldiers.

Milton Lee Olive's memory is being perpetuated by various civic groups. And it should be because his willingness to give to the uttermost stands out as a glaring exception. Milton was a Negro.

It is difficult to discern a man's motives, but in this case, we believe, this act was not an impulsive gesture of heroism for we catch a glimpse of the youth's character from an incident which occurred in the barracks a short time before. Milton was trying to get his bunkmate involved in a discussion on a Bible verse. When his companion registered complete indifference, Milton exclaimed, "Man, you got to care. Believe it or not, you got to care."

He was right on target. If the world in which we walk is miserable and foul, is it not because people do not care? In the story of the Good Samaritan which we can relate so glibly, what is Christ trying to tell us? "Man, you got to care." We have to get involved with the people around us.

We can ponder with profit the epitaph on the headstone of George Washington Carver: "He could have added fortune to fame, but caring for neither, he found happiness and honor in being helpful to the world."

8 PAY THE PRICE*

Two little boys were in deep discussion about the relative merits of their respective fathers. The one, a doctor's son, boasted, "My dad is a doctor and I can be sick for nothing."

"Oh, you think that is something? My father is a minister and I can be good for nothing."

This exchange may explain the lack of virility in our spiritual life. Maybe we are trying to be good "for nothing." Perhaps we are trying to achieve our goal without paying the cost.

Goodness costs something. It demands effort, work, and sacrifice. Nobody can be good "for nothing." Christ minced no words: "If anyone wishes to come after me, let him deny himself and take up his cross and follow me."

Let him deny himself! That is the price. This does not mean crushing normal appetites but controlling them. It does not mean strangling human emotions but subjecting them to reason. It does not mean repressing passions but regulating them. It comes down to this: to salvage, sanctify, and save this soul of ours and to become an effective instrument for the sanctification and salvation of others, we must mortify ourselves.

Mortification is the price of goodness. Mortification is not to be confused with penance. We do penance to make up for the wrong we have done. We mortify ourselves as a spiritual "setting up" exercise. Mortification is a method and means of conditioning and training ourselves. It is moral "gymnastics" to harden the otherwise flabby fiber of our wills and to keep us on the alert against the evil tendencies in our makeup. Mortification is a preventive act. Its purpose is to keep us from doing those things for which we would have to do penance. It does not look to the past but to the present with a keen eye on the future. It is like the premium on fire insurance. We hate to pay it but it certainly pays dividends when fire strikes. We hate to say "no" to our sense of sight and touch and taste and smell, but when the fire of temptation flares up, we stand a better chance of coming through unscathed if we have learned to say "no" in time of relative calm. When we trace the origin of any sin, we find the cause is undue indulgence of one of our senses which can be avenues of mischief. To cope with their demand, I must stay "in condition."

———————
*See *Good Morning, Good People* by Hyacinth Blocker O.F.M.

> *If anyone wants to be a follower of mine, let him re-
> nounce himself and take up his cross and follow me.
> For anyone who wants to save his life will lose it; but
> anyone who loses his life for my sake will find it* (MT.
> 16, 24-25).

9   HELP AT HAND

Have you ever tried to analyze why you go to a certain doctor when you are ill? The reason may very well be because you believe or are lead to believe that this doctor has the necessary skill to help you and more, he wants to help you. Because of this skill and desire, you have confidence in him. It will take a lot of persuading to convince you otherwise. That confidence is firm.

Now, if we have confidence in a man for these reasons, how much more confidence ought we have in God everytime we pray and for the same reasons.

Everything man has, God has in an infinitely perfect degree. God therefore, has the ability to help us. He is omnipotent, all-powerful. All he has to do is will a thing and it is accomplished just because he wills it. St. John writes: "All things were made by him and without him was nothing made." St. Matthew says: "All things are possible to God." Without question God has the ability to help us.

United to this ability is his great love of mankind. In the prayer taught by Christ he instructs us to address God as "Father." He is our heavenly Father and is it not characteristic of a father to have the welfare of his children at heart? Does he not want to help them?

We have ample evidence of the loving care of God. There is so much that we take for granted which actually indicates God's love for us. He had given us our eyes to see, our ears to hear, our legs to walk, our arms to work, our mind to think, our will to love. Everything that we have and everything that we are point to the fatherly care of God.

What is more, Christ bids us: "Ask and you shall receive." Not perhaps, not maybe, not if I am not too busy. We do not have to stand on protocol. But simply "Ask." There is no receptionist at the front door to fend us off; there is no red tape to be cut. He wants it clearly understood that he is willing and anxious to help.

If God has the power and ability to help us; if God is willing and anxious to help us, then by all means we ought to have the greatest confidence in God when we pray. There is everything at hand to engender an unshakable confidence.

"Ask and you shall receive."

Let us be confident, then, in approaching the throne of grace, that we shall have mercy from him and find grace when we are in need of help (HEB. 4, 16).

10 APPRECIATE ONESELF

St. Thomas defines humility as the "reasonable pursuit of one's own excellence." This means, first of all, that we have to recognize we have an inner worth, all of us. There is something wonderful about this creature, man, who was created a little less than the angels, who has the image of God stamped upon him. It is very important that we esteem ourselves. We must learn to appreciate this worth. There is no merit in carrying around a mental picture of ourselves as defeated, deflated, worthless, persons. There is no merit in dramatizing ourselves as objects of pity. This is a false image and complicates life.

It is not egoism to appreciate our own worth unless we foolishly assume that we made ourselves and therefore deserve all the credit. As long as we remember, "not to us, but to thy name give glory," we need have no fear we are on the wrong track. Granting that much, we certainly can and should acknowledge our real assets, and we all have some. Self-appreciation can be wholesome and necessary. Our Lord indicated as much when he made love of self the norm for love of neighbor. "Love your neighbor as you love yourself."

So many people run into trouble not because they love themselves too much but because they love themselves too little. If a person loves himself too much, if he is arrogant and proud, he will soon be taken care of by his peers. They will bring him down to a more realistic level and he will profit in the process.

But a person who does not love himself enough, who does not appreciate his inner worth will be a problem to himself and others. And nobody is able to pump self-esteem into him. This he has to do for himself.

To begin with, we must start with the truth that we are children of God. To be sure no one is perfect, but we all have human dignity with a touch of the divine in it. This we must realize as well as we can, for if we realize that we do have this basic excellence and pursue it with reasonable zeal, we can help ourselves toward maturity and spiritual growth. We are all called to Christian "perfection." This vocation would be pointless and futile if we did not have an "excellence" on which to build.

Didn't you realize that you were God's temple and that the spirit of God was living among you? If anybody should destroy the temple of God, God will destroy him, because the temple of God is sacred; and you are that temple (1 COR. 3, 16-17).

11 MY BROTHER'S KEEPER

They were scaling the Alps together. A doctor and his guide were tied together by a rope. Suddenly, a false step and a slip. The rope held firm, but the two men dangled in mid-air. Their only chance was to cut the rope, but this meant a fatal snip for one of them.

"Your life is worth more than mine," called the guide. He cut the rope and fell. When a searching party found the rope, it still held the doctor, but he was dead. At the bottom of the cliff, they found the guide badly bruised but still alive. A literal illustration of the words of Christ that whoever loses his life saves it. There is, however, a more germane meaning to the words: "For he who would save his life will lose it; but he who loses his life for my sake will find it." In plain language, our Lord is saying, "Get involved."

The levite and the Temple priest by-passed the wounded traveler who fell among robbers. You have noticed they did not want to get involved. Somebody should do something for that poor family down the block. Always somebody, but not I. I don't want to get involved. Somebody ought to do something about the fallen-away Christian. Somebody should do something about the rough teen-agers in the neighborhood, too. And somebody should get the filthy magazines off the stands. There are these and so many other things about which somebody ought to do something. It is always somebody, but not I. I don't want to get involved. I don't want to lose my time, I don't want to lose my convenience and comfort. I don't want to lose my life.

If only we were more aware of our membership in the Mystical Body, perhaps then we would not hesitate to get more involved, even at a price. If I am about to fall on my nose, immediately my hands get involved to break the fall even if they get bruised in the attempt. If I step on a splinter, my eye gets involved looking for the sliver, my fingers get involved trying to pull it out. My bloodstream gets involved to prevent infection. My head does not ignore the foot's injury. We are our brothers' keeper and we ought to get involved. Don't hurry past people in trouble. Do take a moment to help a stranger. Reach out and give of yourself. Don't hoard your time, your talents, and your life merely for yourself. Your life is more worthwhile when shared with others.

> . . . *God put all the separate parts into the body on purpose. If all the parts were the same, how could it be a body. As it is, parts are many but the body is one. The eye cannot say to the hand, 'I do not need you,' nor can the head say to the feet, 'I don't need you'* (1 COR. 12, 18-21).

12 DYNAMIC CHRISTIAN

Where is the magnetism of Christ today? The life of the Church is the life of Christ continued in time. In a sense that can be said of each of us. It is true that we can reproduce the life of Christ only in broken fragments, but the main idea remains; it is our mission to carry on the life of Christ as well as we can.

His life was a life of power. He dominated the elements, "peace, be still" and the storm quieted down. "Lazarus, come forth" and the dead arose. Even his mild speech thrilled with the same tone of power. "He speaks as one having authority." He was dynamic in the fullest and best sense of the abused word. He radiated force. Everything about him possessed character. His influence made itself felt in every way. He draw all eyes toward him. He impelled the indifferent toward him. They had to take sides, one way or the other. They had to be for him or against him. Beyond doubt, no man in history has ever made such a tremendous personal impact upon the people around him.

My original contention is that the mission of the Church is to reproduce the life of Christ. But we are the Church in the little world in which we move. It is up to us then to reproduce the life of Christ.

We must remember, however, that one of the dominant notes in that reproduction must be a dynamic living of the life of Christ. It is a very bad omen if there is a Christian who is unnoticed because his life is so colorless that it neither attracts favor or disfavor. It is a tragic development if a Christian life is so toned down that people discern nothing of the characteristics of Christ, nothing virile, appealing, inspiring, conquering, grand.

He has put all things under his feet, and made him, as ruler of everything, the head of the Church; which is his body, the fullness of him who fills the whole creation (EPH. 1, 22-23).

13 REASSURANCE OF GOD

Unknown to either penitent, the priest had left the confessional and the slide door at each confessional was open. One penitent, unconcerned, rattled through his confession before he noticed the absence of the priest and that the other penitent was listening intently. He stopped abashed and said: "Did you hear what I said?"

"Yeah."

"What do you think?"

"You ought to be in jail."

This conversation focuses attention on a striking contrast. Civil authorities set up courts of justice and ride the letter of the law. God in Confession has set up a court of mercy. This is a consoling fact. Christ comes to us now as a merciful judge so that later he will not have to come as a stern judge. We, therefore, defeat our Savior's purpose if we approach confession as though it were the imposition of a prosecuting attorney anxious to trap us. Christ is no taskmaster and to act as if he were is to misunderstand him.

Confession vindicates the mercy of God. Confession is not necessary to appease the anger of God or to win his pardon. An act of perfect love, an act of perfect contrition brings instant pardon and immediate restoration of God's grace. A truly contrite heart receives pardon just as quickly as the Good Thief.

Confession expresses a human need, not a divine need. It is necessary to satisfy man and not to satisfy God. When Christ instituted confession, he was thinking not of himself but of us. He pardons in a flash and would pardon without further ado if that were good for us. He saw, however, that it would not be good for us to be let off without an apology and an expressed repentance for sin. He wants us to realize the malice of sin. If Christ did not make certain demands, we would surely take sin too lightly. By insisting on a formal oral apology, Christ is preventing us from taking sin for granted. For once we begin to take sin for granted, we are doomed.

In instituting confession, Christ was taking into consideration a very human need. When we have offended God, we want some assurance that our sins have been forgiven. If we were angels, we might dispense with this assurance. To talk to God is one thing, but to be quite certain that God is talking to us, speaking words of pardon and peace, is another thing. We sense a deep contentment when Christ through his spokesman says: "Go in peace. Your sins are forgiven you."

Though your sins are like scarlet, they shall be as white as snow; though they be as red as crimson, they shall be like wool (Isa. 1, 18).

14   BREAD OF LIFE

A movement of unrest rippled through the crowd. What they had just heard bothered their common sense. Some of the people quietly slipped away from the crowd, ashamed to have been there in the first place. Others huddled together in whispering consternation. The words that so disturbed the crowd were still ringing in their ears. "I am the bread of life. I am the living bread that came down from heaven. If anyone eat of this bread, he will live forever. And the bread that I give is my flesh for the life of the world." This happened along the sea of Galilee near the city of Capharnum.

"How can this man give us his flesh to eat?" Notice that the argument did not center about the meaning of the words of Christ but rather about how he was going to make good his words. There was no question that Christ had promised to give his real flesh as food. That is how his words were understood and that is exactly how Christ wanted those words understood. He reaffirms his position: "Unless you eat the flesh of the Son of Man and drink his blood, you shall not have life in you." The promise is clear.

The fulfillment is just as clear. "While they were at supper, Jesus took bread and blessed and broke and gave it to the disciples and said: 'Take and eat. This is my body.' And taking the cup he gave thanks and gave it to them, saying, 'All of you drink this for this is my blood which is being shed for many unto the forgiveness of sins.' "

What Jesus offered to his apostles then had the appearance of bread and wine that he picked up from the table a moment before. Yet his words are unmistakable. The seeming bread and wine that he now offers them, he tells us in the plainest of plain words, are his body and blood. To interpret these words in any other manner is to do violence to the obvious meaning of the words.

How this change takes place Christ had not seen fit to tell us. He was under no obligation to do so. That it does take place we do know with a knowledge that is more certain than scientific analysis for it is based upon the infallible authority of God. We take Christ's word for it. After all, he gave to wine its redness and taste; he gave to bread its brittleness and shape and taste. By multiplying loaves and converting water into wine, he showed his power over bread and wine. Why then should he not be able to give a new substance under identical appearances? Why not be able to retain the redness of the wine and the brittleness of the bread, why not be able to retain the size, the color, the taste and shape of bread, the color and taste of wine as a mask and come himself to hide behind them?

That is exactly what happened when the transubstantiation occurred when Christ spoke the words of consecration on the night before he died. He gave us his body and blood under the appearance of bread and wine.

For my flesh is real food and my blood is real drink.
He who eats my flesh and drinks my blood lives in
me and I live in him (JN. 6, 55-57).

15 SECRET SAMARITANS

There are some people who must always hold the center of the stage. They will not engage in any enterprise unless all eyes are upon them. When they discharge a duty, the report must be heard around the world. If the seventy-six trombones are not at hand to head the big parade, they will not stir a finger.

Our Lord met up with this kind of character. He had some severe words for them: "Take heed not to do your good before men, in order to be seen by them; otherwise you shall have no reward with your Father in heaven. Therefore when thou givest alms, do not sound the trumpet before thee, as the hypocrites do in the synogogues and streets in order that they may be honored by men. Amen, I say to you, they have received their reward. But when thou givest alms, do not let thy left hand know what thy right hand is doing, so that thy alms may be given in secret; and thy Father who sees in secret will reward thee."

If more of us paid attention to these words, I am sure that more good would be done in the world. So much good is left undone because we are so concerned about who will get the credit.

The person who has not tried to do some good on the sly does not know what joy he is missing. There is a special kind of satisfaction that comes from doing good and keeping it secret.

Recently I read of a man in Boston who came to an understaffed orphanage every Wednesday afternoon to spend several hours entertaining the youngsters with tricks and stories and whatnot. The staff had no idea who he was, but the instant he appeared, he was greeted with shouts of joy. When people tried to probe and discover his identity, he would only say: "That is not important."

The art of doing good and doing it in secret does not come naturally. It must be cultivated because it goes against one of the stronger hungers in our makeup, the hunger for recognition and approval of others. When people do not notice our good deeds, we are always tempted subtly to call attention to them.

Once we cultivate the art of doing good in secret, we are amazed at how much more good we do just because we don't care who gets the credit.

But when you give alms, your left hand must not know what your right is doing; your almsgiving must be secret, and your Father who sees all that is done in secret will reward you (MT. 6, 3-4).

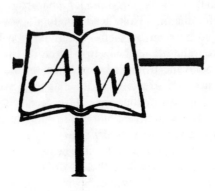

16   PUBLIC RELATIONS

This day of ecumenism can learn a lot from the greatest of all missionaries, St. Paul. He is perhaps one of the most outstanding examples of good public relations. He did not compromise the truth, ever, but neither did he ride roughshod over the religious sensibilities of others. What prompted his every action was a sincere love of people. Because he loved people he was afire with a desire to share Christ and Christ's truth with them.

One day at Athens while waiting for his co-workers to catch up with him, he was deeply moved by what he observed. "His heart was moved within him to find the city so much given over to idolatry." He made his way to the business district where he could get in direct contact with the people. He struck up a conversation with everyone he met. Paul was a "good mixer." He kept moving deeper into their midst until finally they decided to give him a public hearing.

Now notice his approach. His opening words were a masterpiece of tender regard for the feelings of others who had beliefs directly opposed to his own. He had noticed the innumerable altars and even one erected to the "unknown God." He acknowledged their inclination toward religion. He accepted the fact that these people were, as he said, "scrupulously religious." He calls attention to the altar of the unknown God and states he has come to tell them about that unknown God.

St. Paul was not very successful on this particular occasion, but the incident does point up an attitude that is important in our day when religion is being discussed more freely. Paul felt that he had to adapt himself to the people and not expect the people to conform to him. He strove hard not to offend. He was not trying to prove how wrong they were and how right he was. He was not out to beat them down or hurt them in any way. On the contrary he went to great lengths to indicate every possible area of agreement. He went to them and did not expect them to come to him. He was out to impart knowledge and not win an argument. It is this kind of attitude that must govern our thinking in these days of ecumenism.

> *Be tactful with those who are not Christian and be sure you make the best use of your time with them. Talk to them agreeably and with a flavor of wit and try to fit your answers to the needs of each one* (COL. 4, 4-6).

17   COOL IT

One of the most overused devices is the panic button. The reason often is because we distort reality. Many problems that confront us can be solved in a simple and unexpected manner if we keep our heads.

Some sailors, we are told, drifted off course and were dying of thirst. At long last they sighted another vessel. They were miles from shore and it appeared that a broken rudder would not bring them close enough to launch a small rescue boat.

"Water!" They signalled desperately. "Send us water!"

The other boat returned the message: "Drop your buckets in the ocean and take all the water you need."

This seemed a cruel jest for they had tried the water before and found it salty, sure to kill. Finally they were convinced to let their buckets down. They brought them up filled with fresh, sweet water. Unknown to them, they had drifted to the very mouth of the Amazon where fresh water empties into the sea. Their problem was solved in a simple and unexpected way.

One day the bassoon player frantically approached Toscanini minutes before the symphony was to begin. He was panicky because his instrument could not reach E-flat. The conducter bent his head deep in thought for a moment then said: "That is quite all right. E-flat does not occur in your music for this number." The problem was solved in a simple and unexpected way.

We all have problems. But why push the panic button? This merely confuses the issue. Let us stop right where we are and take a good look at what is happening now and respond only to what is happening now. Let's ask ourselves, "What is there here and now that I have to respond to? What can I do about *that*?" A great deal of panic is caused by trying to do something here and now which need not be done here and now. In many cases we are automatically reacting not to the present moment but to a similar situation of the past. So we are not reacting to reality but to a fiction. We are fighting strawmen, jousting with windmills.

If you have a tiger by the tail, if you are on the endless treadmill of worry, if you are swamped by problems, don't lose sight of reality. Don't overreact. Keep your head and the solution may come in a simple and unexpected manner.

> *The trials that you have to bear are no more than normal people have. You can trust God not to let you be tried beyond your strength, and with any trial he will give you a way out of it and the strength to bear it* (1 Cor. 10, 13).

18   LIVING WORD

Francis of Assisi presented a strange image as he cut across the trend of his times. The cross scrawled on the back of his coarse garment indicated how completely he intended to conform his life to the principles of the Gospel. He accepted the Gospel message as if addressed to him personally.

The Gospel was, after all, a pattern for living. Christ did not intend for his message to be printed between two covers and gather dust on the shelves. He wanted that message to take on flesh and blood, and live and move among men.

This is exactly what Francis wanted also. And at first the people thought he was a "nut." Determined, he pursued his purpose. When the sincerity of his endeavor became apparent, the crowds began to flock after him. It was then that Francis made a bold move. He leaped over monastery walls and brought his way of life to the people. He set down a simple way of life leading directly to the love of God. He made this way of life available to every condition of life, every age and both sexes without breaking family bonds or household ties. Since then thousands of people have attempted to walk the path traced out by Francis of Assisi.

But what started it all? A life, a human, vibrant, warm life! Francis did not envision a world-wide movement. In the beginning he did not look beyond the limits of his own personality. He as much as said: "I know the world is in a bad way, therefore I will begin with myself." He was perceptive enough to realize that society ultimately is persons. So he did not begin with institutions or parties or unions. He began with a person, namely himself, knowing full well that the world can be improved only by multiplying personal reforms. He wanted to steep himself so full of goodness that like a reservoir he could not help spilling over.

It was this spilling over of the goodness within him that attracted the people around him. They drew their inspiration from the personal experience of seeing the heights to which human effort could rise. Francis took up from there and led these people back to the source of his own initial inspiration which was Christ and his Gospel message. Can it be that we touch upon the secret of the success of the Little Man of Assisi?

And the one who received the seed in rich soil is the man who hears the word and understands it; he is the one who yields a harvest and produces now a hundredfold, now sixty, now thirty (Mt. 13, 23).

19   LIGHT AND LOVE

In a few words at the end of "Pacem in Terris" Pope John XXIII give us an idea of the essence of Christianity. The more we meditate on these words and the more we attempt to exemplify them in our own lives, the more effectively we will fulfill our role as Christians.

"Every believer in this world of ours," writes the recent Pope, "must be a spark of light, a center of love, a vivifying leaven amidst his fellowmen; and he will be this all the more perfectly, the more closely he lives in communion with God in the intimacy of his soul."

A spark of light
A center of love
A vivifying leaven
In union with Christ

In the gloomy darkness around us a Christian must stand out as a spark of light showing the way to truth which leads back to God. This means that he must know and understand what he believes so he can give a reasonable account of his belief. Not only must he know, he must also live his faith because what we are is so much more eloquent than what we say.

The effectiveness of this "spark of light" will depend on our degree of love. We must be centers of love. Love must be the very essence of our existence. It must be a force in our lives, compelling, urging, driving. It must give us no rest, no respite. We must have something of the spirit of Paul who was jet-propelled by love.

If we are a spark of light and a center of love, we can't help being a vivifying leaven in society. Every person has an influence for good or for evil. This is unavoidable. The more we abound with truth, the more we are filled with love, the greater is our influence for good. If we can multiply the number of people working for good, society will be a better place. Each one must pull his share.

The touchstone for all this is union with Christ: union with Christ through grace, union with Christ through prayer, union with Christ through the sacraments, union with Christ through imitation.

The more intimately our life is bound up with the life and spirit of Christ, the more effective we become as a source of "light and love and leaven."

> *You were darkness once, but now you are light in the Lord; be like children of light, for the effects of light are seen in complete goodness and right living and truth. Try to discover what the Lord wants of you, having nothing to do with the futile works of darkness but exposing them by contrast* (EPH. 5, 8-11).

20 STEPPING STONES

There is no question that material goods, their acquisition and use occupy large chunks of our waking moments. In America especially, industry like a giant womb is spawning gadget after gadget to ease the bumps on the road of life. No matter where we turn creature comforts worm their way into our manner of living. Certainly something that is so much a part of our living in this world, must have some bearing on our living in the next world. The recent Constitution on the Church took note of this relationship. It warns: "Let neither the use of the things of this world nor attachment to riches, which is against the spirit of evangelical poverty, hinder them in their quest for perfect love."

To be imbued with this spirit it is necessary to disengage our hearts from the things of this world even though we have to provide prudently for the future.

Didn't St. Francis have the correct idea? He held material goods at arm's length. Not because he hated these goods as some would have us believe, but precisely because he loved them. He loved them so much that he would allow them to fulfill the purpose for which God created them, namely to lead man back to God. This, after all, is the essence of true love. To lead to God. This purpose cannot be served if we allow material goods to so entangle our hearts that they strangle our efforts to get back to God.

Of course, there can be no quarrel with material goods. We need them. But the big question is: how do we use them? Do we make them our little tin gods, as if nothing else in the world mattered? Every morning newspaper carries stories of people who do just that, prefer material possessions to God. This is evident because they do not hesitate to violate the law of God in order to lay hold of some portion of this perishable earth.

Are we immune from this tendency? Do we not at times betray the purpose of God's creatures? Whenever we do, they become stumbling blocks instead of stepping stones. In every use of material things our norm ought to be this: are we getting closer to God through this creature?

> *Get yourselves purses that do not wear out, treasure that will not fail you, in heaven where no thief can reach it and no moth destroy it. For where your treasure is, there will your heart be also* (LK. 12, 33-34).

21 DON'T BE HAMSTRUNG

"You are my God, teach me to do your will." St. Francis often said this short meaningful prayer. In the Our Father we express the same sentiments. "Thy will be done on earth as it is in heaven." There is little doubt that all of us want God's will to be realized in our lives and the lives of those around us. But what is God's will in the give and take of daily living? This is the rub.

Is it whatever happens in my life? Many good people think they have to stand mute and helpless in any circumstances. They scruple if they detect agitation within themselves to change things. Well, the fact is some things can be changed and should be changed.

There is a whole lot of sense in the AA motto: "God, give me the serenity to accept the things I cannot change, the courage to change the things that I can and the good sense to know the difference."

Proper order, this is an indication of God's will. If a person is the victim of injustice and there is no compelling reason like charity, why should it be tolerated? It is not against God's will that we protest and try to change it. It could even be a failing to stand there with bowed head and say, "God has allowed this to happen to me so it must be that he wills I endure it."

What we forget is that God has also given us brains and the ability in some instances to alter conditions, to fit things into right order. If this is possible, it is just good sense for man to give form and direction to the world about him in keeping with his powers. If I have an emotional makeup that creates great anxiety within me, I must not say: This is my cross and I have to bear it. If something can be done with reasonable effort, I ought to do it. This holds true in any case.

On the other hand there are some things over which a person has no control. If it rains, what can I do about it other than get in out of the rain? There are limits to what I can do. Things of this nature we must embrace as God's permissive will. So it is a matter of distinguishing.

You are slaves to no one except God, so behave like free men . . . (1 PET. 2, 16).

22   LET THERE BE LIGHT

When the east coast suffered its power failure and blackout, the one thing uppermost in the minds of most people was — where can I get some light! All of a sudden light had become the most important commodity. When it was on hand, people had taken it very much for granted. In the blackout they began to realize its value.

Human ingenuity devised incredible means of producing light for the emergency. One office dispatched a janitor to a nearby church. After making a substantial contribution, he returned with all the vigil lights. (The Church as a source of light makes an interesting parable.)

Darkness has always been the virtual enemy of man. When illness strikes, we long for the first rays of dawn. We become anxious when groping in the dark. Imprisonment in total darkness is a severe punishment. The ultimate in punishment is the "exterior darkness" referred to in Sacred Scripture. We want light; we need light!

But there is a darkness other than darkness of the eyes. There is also darkness of the mind. One of the results of the fall of man was a "darkening of our intellect." From the moment he awakens to consciousness man is engaged in the perennial struggle to dissipate this darkness. His constant struggle is to push back the frontiers of darkness to let in a little light of truth. We have elaborated a huge educational system for that very purpose. Deepseated in our nature is a craving for this light of the mind, which is truth. So natural is this striving that the person who is no longer struggling to attain it has betrayed his purpose. The search goes on unremittingly because there is in man a hunger that will not be satisfied with anything less than Truth itself.

There is a darkness other than darkness of the mind. There is also darkness of the soul. We grieve for the man who walks with unsure foot, in agony lest he make a misstep. Life can be a torture without a guiding light to direct our way. Many stumble in their moral life because they have closed their eyes to the true Light.

Christ made a big issue of the point: "I am the light of the world. He who follows me does not walk in darkness but will have the light of life." Can it be that we are missing the obvious? Our search for truth and light is really a search for Christ. Man's struggle to provide light for the eyes should be a healthy reminder that he needs light for the mind and light for the soul as well.

> *Walk while you have the light, or the dark will over-take you; he who walks in the dark does not know where he is going. While you still have the light, be-lieve in the light and you will become sons of light* (JN. 12, 35-36).

23   SERVICE STATION

Service to others is very much a matter of attitude. We allow so many opportunities of being of service to others go by unrecognized for the simple reason that we are not attuned to the people around us.

If our thoughts are forever turning inward upon ourselves, we will be of little service to others just because helping them does not fit into our scheme of things.

It is important that we develop a sensitivity, an awareness of people. It is important in the Christian concept that we broaden our horizon. It is so cozy and comfortable to shut ourselves up in our ivory towers and let the rest of the world go by. But is it Christian?

The temple priest and the levite intent on their own purposes pass by a man dying by the wayside. They lacked an openness to people. Their attitude prevented them from being of service.

We keep coming back to that same idea — service to others is a matter of attitude. Perhaps the trouble with too many of us is the fact that we keep asking, "What's in it for me?" If we cannot see some immediate or even a definite future gain, we are not interested.

Perhaps we are suffering from myopia. We can't see beyond our nose. We can't see that this is no ordinary flesh and blood that we ignore. This is "a member of the household of God and a citizen with the saints." It comes down to measuring life in terms of eternity and not personal aggrandizement.

Only if we recognize Christ in our neighbor, will we be reminded to extend ourselves even to the point of discomfort and inconvenience. This kind of recognition can alter our attitude and dispose us to be of service.

But there is the rub. Maybe we are not taking seriously the clear wording of Scripture: "Saul, Saul, why are you persecuting me? Now you are the body of Christ, member for member. As long as you did it to the least of my brethren, you did it to me."

> *Do not let your love be a pretense, but sincerely prefer good to evil. Love each other as much as brothers should, and have a profound respect for each other. Work for the Lord with untiring effort and with great earnestness of spirit. If any of the saints are in need you must share with them; and you should make hospitality your special care* (ROM. 12, 9-13).

24   WIDE AWAKE

Grace builds on nature. Grace does not destroy nature. God is the author of both and he does not destroy the work of his hand. Suppose we are irascible and short-tempered, suppose we are shy and retiring, suppose we are temperamental and sensitive, suppose we are prone to impurity — what of it? Grace takes us as we are, the irascible, the meek, the intrepid, the affectionate, and elevates, ennobles and gently bends us. This petty earth-clinging soul can be raised to the heights.

Grace, however, wants a wide-awake, alert reception. Grace wants enthusiasm!

Wherever grace meets with enthusiasm, we find holiness. There are still a lot of holy people in the world. There are thousands of people who rub shoulders with sin in our crowded street cars and busses, in our workshops and offices. They are not besmirched by the contagion. There are good clean men in our workshops; there are pure virtuous girls in our offices; there are self-sacrificing mothers and dutiful fathers. And these people are such because they have more enthusiasm for God than for sinful alluring pleasure. There are many young people in the world who preserve their innocence despite contact with evil. They can dance, play cards, go places and do interesting and decent things, and the next morning you see them at the Communion rail.

They have a zest for living. But in the swirl of the dance, in their quest for fun they reserved some of their enthusiasm for God. That is why in our twentieth century we have our saints, our little saints. If we look for it, we can see sanctity eddying around the corners, dwelling in the hovels of the poor, living in the mansions of the wealthy, poring over books, editing a school paper, pecking at a typewriter. These are people who know the exciting, exhilarating, scintillating experience of the fullness of life because they are enthusiastic for the things that count.

It was this youthful bubbling over, this fervid effervesence that accounts for the gallant action of St. Francis of Assisi as he sallies forth a confident troubador of Christ. See the glowing enthusiasm of St. Ignatius as his fiery nature bids his followers conquer the world for Christ. See the enthusiasm of St. Francis Xavier as he brushes aside the glamor of a promising brilliant teaching career to set sail for the far-flung shores of India. Grace built on the affectionate lyrical nature of St. Francis of Assisi, the agressive militaristic nature of St. Ignatius, and the ardent sporting nature of Francis Xavier. In these lives, grace found enthusiasm.

What has become of the enthusiasm you had (GAL. 4, 15)?
As long as the day lasts I must carry out the work of the one who sent me; the night will soon be here when no man can work (JN. 9, 4).

25   LET IN THE LIGHT

I bruised my shins against an open drawer because I chose to grope in the darkness instead of turning on the light. This was stupid of me. Did I learn my lesson? Not quite. I also bumped my nose against the door. Save your sympathy because I heal quickly. However, it is no laughing matter when I reflect that this is the way I often conduct my spiritual life. I grope around in the darkness and keep bumping into the same sins and tripping over the same commandments. You would think I would learn my lesson and let in a little light. Maybe I am afraid to light up the hidden recesses of my conscience. Perhaps I dread the unveiling of sordid motives and evil tendencies which self-love conveniently shadows over. It is not always a happy experience to meet your real self in the glare of an honest scrutiny. Can I really be serious about this business of bettering myself if I refuse to take a good look at myself? If I never learn my weaknesses, I go through life shadow-boxing. That seems to be a foolish way to spend my energies.

Because I tend to shy away from the pain of self-discovery, I need the discipline of a way of life that binds me to the obligation of a daily examination of conscience. To insure fidelity I must determine the exact time and place. I must also settle on a definite method of procedure. I have to stop kidding myself that the pace of my life is so hectic that I can't work out some semblance of routine.

It is like pausing to look at a map. I find my present location, seek out my destination; then go. The important thing is to go. But reading that map gives confidence that we are headed in the right direction. In other words, the examination of conscience is merely a means to the higher goal of deepening my love of God and neighbor. To be effective, it must be consistent and enduring. This is why I am counseled to take a good look each day. It just makes good sense to save myself from bruised shins and battered noses by letting in a little light.

26   GOD'S HELPER

During his pontificate Pope Paul VI was preoccupied with the role of the layman in the modern Church. Rooted firmly in solid traditions, his was a forward looking position.

"Those who dedicate themselves to render Catholic testimony must nourish in themselves the knowledge, the reality, and in a certain sense the consciousness of a live and personal contact with Christ, by means of grace, that is by means of a supernatural relationship, in order to experience in themselves and to show others that their faith is not a conventional display of given forms of thought, or custom and of ritual, but a vital principle which bestows absolute sincerity on their religious profession, a personal conviction, an intimate source of goodness, of vigor and of joy, and an interior exuberance which overflows into the exterior charity, to which we gave the name 'apostolate.' "

Pope Paul says so much in that brief statement that one could spend hours probing the depth and breadth of its meaning. Notice how he gets to the core of the matter immediately — works of the apostolate must be an overflow of the inner strength of an ardent spiritual life. "Overflow" is the key word. This makes one wonder about the action groups in the Church which seem to claim that the spiritual life is built up by complete immersion in the active life. Aren't we somehow expecting wine without crushing the grapes?

Certainly we have no quarrel with expectation that the laymen assume his rightful role in the life and work of the Church. This is a development every thinking person yearns to witness. But are we not expecting some minor miracle of grace if we anticipate finding competent laymen, made to order, to fill the many roles the Church has in mind. They simply do not just drop from heaven. Everybody starts as a helpless infant. Somehow, somewhere, we all must get a chance to develop our spiritual life at least to the point where our work in and with the Church is an overflow of deep spirituality. Otherwise we run a serious risk of fouling up the work of the Church. It is not merely competency that the Church needs in her laymen but a special kind of competency, rather a competency imbued with a special spirit. One of the means that has effectively trained many souls in that special spirit through the centuries has been the Third Orders.

> *Go, therefore, make disciples of all nations baptize them in the name of the Father and of the Son and of the Holy Spirit, and teach them to observe all the commands I gave you. And know that I am with you always; yes, to the end of time* (MT. 28, 19-20).

27   DON'T BE A ROBOT

Are you in a rut? Most of us are. Day after day we do the same routine things in the same old routine way. We loathe to change the pattern because it just wouldn't feel right. So we go along in our dull, monotonous, uninteresting way. This is true of life in general; it is true of the spiritual life in particular.

Perhaps I am an unorthodox retreatmaster, but whenever I give a retreat, I advise the retreatants to leave their prayerbooks at home. If they make the way of the cross, I suggest they start with the fourteenth station. I tell them to say the rosary backwards. The idea is to get them to perform their religious exercises in a way entirely different from the way they are accustomed to performing them.

We don't always have to say the same dull insipid prayers before Holy Communion. We don't always have to gain the indulgence after Communion by reciting the prayer before the crucifix. Do we always have to confess our sins in the same order, using identical language from confession to confession? There are other ways of attending Mass than using the missal, or our First Communion prayerbook.

What we are saying is this: if we can deliberately jerk ourselves out of the rut we are in, we may see the elements of our spiritual life in a different light. We may gain new insights. We may be inspired to greater fervor. Most probably we will fall back into the old routine, but at least for the moment we have experienced something different.

In any event we must understand that routine tends to kill devotion. It makes us perfunctory and mechanical. It stifles the spontaneity of relating to God in a personal way. And this ought to be the main endeavor of our spiritual striving — a personal response to the grace of God. I feel that the less we use pat formulas, the more personal this response can become.

The current change in the liturgy is an attempt on the part of the Church to thaw the congealed, rigid, even impersonal manner of worship. She wants to engage the human personality more completely and intimately. We may not like the changes, because any change of pattern in personal devotion or public worship is a strange experience. We don't have to like the changes and I'm sure there are many people who don't. But we cannot dispute the intent of the Church which in plain language is — get out of the rut.

This people honors me only with lip service, while their hearts are far from me. The worship they offer is worthless; the doctrines they teach are only human regulations (MT. 15, 8-9).

28 THE BEAUTY OF SANCTITY

The spiritual life that we present to young people must be level-headed and sane. There seems to be a strange twist in the thinking of young people whereby they associate the spiritual life with stuffiness. As a rule they are quite tolerant of epithets, but if you want to make them fidget and squirm, tell them they are pious. Somehow that strikes a tender spot. They have gotten it into their heads that piety makes them some kind of monster. We have to disabuse them of this misconception. That is why our ideals must be presented as something sensible and sane. We have to demonstrate that piety is supernatural common sense. There has to be a sound naturalness and a natural soundness.

Second, simplicity. Like all truly great things, the spiritual life must be simple. We have to be lucid, clearcut and unaffected. Certainly the spiritual life is sublime but let's not confuse sublimity with complexity. An ideal can be sublime without being complex. We have to make it clear that the spiritual life does not consist in a multitude of devotional practices. They simply will not tolerate being enmeshed in a network of multiple rules and regulations. When you come right down to it, multiple devotions menace genuine piety and degrade it to a soulless formalism. Has it ever struck us that Our Lord reduced the whole field of the spiritual life to one word — love? Love presupposes knowledge, love begets service.

Third, virility. By this term we want to rule out whatever is purely emotional. There are certain coarser elements in the spiritual life than cannot be ignored. That is why it is fatal to allow the young people to be guided by mood and feeling and emotion instead of by conviction, duty, and obligation. It is true that there is a certain amount of warmth that may accompany practices of piety. We must take care, however, lest these shadows be mistaken for the substance.

Finally, the brand of spirituality we try to sell our young people must contain unmistakable elements of cheerfulness and joy. Nothing is more alien to Christian spirituality than bleakness and glumness. Despite that fact there are some who believe that entering religion and a program of spiritual effort is tantamount to a cessation of joy and happiness. Those who deal with young people must be personal example that the opposite is true. It is futile to wax eloquent about joy in the service of the Lord and then wend our weary way through life like an accident looking for a place to happen. Real sanctity has no traffic with world-weary pessimism, with that dark and gloomy melancholy that views life through a jaundiced eye.

> *Not that I have become perfect yet: I have not yet won, but I am still running, trying to capture the prize for which Christ Jesus captured me* (PHIL. 3, 12).

29   STICK WITH IT*

It does get discouraging at times, doesn't it? We get our fill of this spiritual combat and wrestling with evil and want to call it quits. What's the point of all this sweat when there is so little evidence of progress. We wake up each morning — to what? The same old grind, the same old struggle. Besides, all the other people seem to be having such a good time without the strain of battle. Here we are in agony trying to walk the straight and narrow.

Join the crowd. You are normal. We all feel the weariness of the struggle. At times we all have to grind out through clenched teeth our acts of faith and hope and love. We all get tired of the uphill fight. So what's your beef? You are as normal as the rest of us. That is the price we have to pay for being human.

It is not so much that our spine has turned to jelly. It is not so much that we lack backbone. More than anything else it is a lack of vision. We are looking in the wrong direction. We are concentrating too much upon ourselves. If I limit my horizon to this pitiful creature — me, it is no wonder at all that I should get discouraged. I know my weaknesses, my limitations. If this is all I see, why should I continue "beating my brains against the hard pavement of reality?"

There is still God, you know.

"But he seems so far away. You can't pray. You are putty in the face of temptation and are ashamed to get close to God." Is this what you are saying?

Be assured that at times like these you are much closer to God than you may imagine. It is not a matter of thinking about God, nor feeling his nearness nor even actually praying that is important. What is important is wanting God, wanting to be near him, wanting to pray, wanting to resist temptation. You are not in serious trouble until you give up even wanting. But as long as you really and sincerely want these things you are in pretty good shape. If you want to be good and are trying to be good, in the measure that you are wanting and trying, you are good.

The moment we say, "What's the use; I quit," we are in serious trouble. The moment we give up wanting and trying and let discouragement take full sway, we will go from bad to worse. It will, in the end, require some minor miracle of grace to lift us up. And we don't come by miracles that easily.

The Latin adage should be our motto: *"Dum spiro, spero."* As long as I can breathe there is still reason to hope for the best.

---

*See *Your Way to God* by Kilian McGowan C.P.

> *So stand your ground, with truth buckled round your waist, and integrity for a breastplate, wearing for shoes on your feet the eagerness to spread the gospel of peace and always carrying the shield of faith so that you can use it to put out the burning arrows of the evil one* (EPH. 6, 14-15).

30   BE CAREFUL

The policeman in this life and hell in the next — these are the motives that govern people without conscience. They are driven by fear. In their eyes there is only one disaster, the disaster of getting caught. But even this is becoming merely an occupational hazard today. Be that as it may, no one in his right mind would dare to rely on such a person. We constantly question the sincerity of his words and the trustworthiness of his actions. For the simple reason that he has no conscience.

Hamlet missed the point when he said, "thus conscience doth make cowards of us all." It is the lack of an upright conscience that makes us cowards, traitors, and turncoats. The man with a well-formed conscience has character.

The person with an upright conscience directing his life inspires confidence. We do not hesitate to trust him. We rely upon him without a trace of anxiety because we know he is exact in fulfilling his duty. His life is characterized by strict sincerity and rigid honesty.

A man of conscience will say: "This charge has been given me not by men but by God. If what I do pleases men, well and good. If people misunderstand or misjudge what I do, I will not stifle conscience just to escape censure. I will do what I am supposed to do regardless of the consequence. No one may value it. No one may know the trouble I have taken. So what? I can look the world squarely in the eye because I have been true to myself."

A man of conscience is touchy, in a way. He will not tolerate disagreement and disharmony between his thoughts and actions. He rebels against underhanded methods that other people call clever. He will not defer to human respect because of a cynical smile or a bit of chafing.

Anything we entrust to a man of conscience is safe, be it possessions, confidential information or even one's reputation. Unless a person has an upright conscience, it does little good to bind his hands or seal his lips, because if his conscience is not right, he will devise means to untie his hands and loose his tongue.

Unfortunately we cannot mass-produce an upright conscience. This little "spark of celestial fire" is planted in the human heart, but it takes individual effort to keep it alive. We have to work at it to sustain a keen awareness of what is right and what is wrong and thus to become fit instruments for the wholesome and good.

31   MEASURE OF LOVE

On the occasion of the Last Supper Christ said: "A new commandment I give you, that you love one another; that as I have loved you, you also love one another. By this will all men know that you are my disciples, if you have love for one another."

Are we disciples of Christ just because we are baptized? Or because we belong to this or that particular religion-oriented group? It is possible to be condemned precisely because of these reasons. Baptism (with the obvious exceptions of infants), membership in the Church or dedication in a religious group do not automatically guarantee discipleship.

Discipleship of Christ is determined in one way: "if you love one another as I have loved you." In the intimacy of his leave-taking, in the company of his select few, Christ adds a new dimension. This was only eighteen hours before his death. Formerly he had said, "Love your neighbor as you love yourself." But this has to be taken in context. At that time he was addressing Scribes and Pharisees and generally non-believers. But now that he is speaking to intimates he completes the idea that would have been lost on his audience before.

"As I have loved you." This is the standard for his inner circle. We are to love our neighbor not only as we love ourselves, because that can be selfishly motivated. Rather we are to love our neighbor as Christ loved us. This is the distinguishing mark of discipleship.

How has Christ loved us? Remember, we are a short time away

from the crucifixion when Christ gathered his followers around the table. He knew what was in store for him and he wants to leave no room for doubt or misunderstanding. "Greater love than this no one has, that one lay down his life for his friends." As soon as he sets this high standard, he leaves the upper room and ascends the heights of Calvary.

Calvary then is the measure of the love that Christ manifests toward us. Christ came to show us how to love and the ultimate example of that love is crucifixion.

The measure of love then that sets the follower of Christ apart from the rest of the world is love to the point of crucifixion. Can we really claim to be true followers of Christ unless we are minded to go the limit? "As I have loved you." This means a love that does not shrink from sacrifice, even bloody, brutal sacrifice for our neighbor. This certainly is not child's play. But there it stands as clear as sunlight "as I have loved you."

> *The life I now live in this body I live in faith; faith in the Son of God who loved me and sacrificed himself for my sake* (GAL. 2, 21).

32   EMMANUEL

With each passing year we seem to cling more tenaciously to Christmas. We begin our celebration long before Christmas itself and hang on until the pine needles drop from the trees and the wreaths wilt. Can it be that the world in which we live is trying to make up for the cold indifference of that first Christmas night? The thought may be more sanguine than realistic, because in most cases the birthday of Christ swiftly dawns and just as swiftly passes and we find ourselves in the groove of work-a-day living.

But need it be so, especially for those who believe in the Eucharistic presence of Christ? If we think about it on this basis, every day is Christmas.

As we reflect on the first Christmas night, we recall the simplicity and the mystery of the occasion. It was a time when our God and Savior came to earth. It was the end of our aloneness and the beginning of God-with-us. Christ left the tabernacle of his mother's womb because "his delight was to be with the children of men." This very same thing happens every day on our altars. Day after day Christ returns to take his place among us. He leaves the tabernacle of heaven to come to earth and then he leaves the tabernacle of the altar to come to our hearts. Every union with Christ is Christmas all over again.

Had we lived in the time of Christ, would we have been on hand to welcome the newborn King? Would we have been fortunate enough to hear the good news of great joy? And if we had heard it, would we have done anything about it? Would we have found the stable and the crib? Would we have recognized Christ in the swaddling clothes? It is quite possible we would have been creatures of our times chained to our beds, our comfort, our unbelief. It would have been a Christmas without Christ.

We, however, have been born in an age of faith, weak though it may be. We are the fortunate heirs of the devoted ages of faith. Ours is the heritage of believers and that is why we can make the transition from Bethlehem to the tabernacle without strain. We can experience the wonderful traditions of Christmas carried on in the Eucharist. It is our task then to pass on these traditions, fortified and purified, so that every generation after us will know the joy of the good news, Emmanuel, God-with-us!

> *He came to his own domain and his own people did not accept him. But to all who did accept him he gave power to become children of God . . .* (JN. 1, 11-12).

33 UNIQUE DIGNITY

"If anyone loves me, he will keep my word and my Father will love him and we will come to him and make our abode with him."

When we were baptized the priest prayed: "Depart, unclean spirit, from this creature fashioned by God whom our Lord has deigned to call unto his temple so that he may become a temple of the living God and that the Holy Spirit may dwell in him." Could we but see the marvelous transformation that took place then, we would get down on our knees in adoration before the God who comes into our heart. "Know you not," cries St. Paul in an effort to make us realize our dignity, "know you not that you are the temple of God and the spirit of God dwells in you?"

If the Holy Spirit dwells in us in a special way, then certainly we ought to have a reverent regard for his dwelling place. A noble mind recoils from the knowledge that a church has been profaned or desecrated. Our Lord himself gave vent to just anger when he noticed that the house of his Father was turned into a den of thieves. If the profanation of a physical temple is repugnant to God, how much more repugnant to see one of his living temples desecrated by sin. Let us then live up to our dignity!

If we live up to our dignity as a child of God and preserve unmarred the temple of the Holy Spirit, we will come into our inheritance, the glory of the life to come.

There is a unique relationship between our life of grace in this world and our life of glory in the next. St. Thomas calls grace "the beginning of glory." Heaven is in grace as an oak is in an acorn. It is there in embryo. Heaven is nothing more than the blossoming into full bloom of our life of sanctifying grace.

If we understood this fact, we might be more concerned about our supernatural life of grace. If we could begin to grasp the honor, the nobility, the riches, and beauty that go with sanctifying grace, we would certainly be convinced there is more to life than merely living it.

To be a follower of Christ means, first and foremost, to be a supernatural being. A Christian in the fullest sense is someone who has been raised to God's level by aptitudes, powers, and privileges that are above nature. A Christian in the fullest sense of the term is not living up to his calling unless his efforts revolve around the supernatural life of grace — acquiring it, preserving it, and increasing it.

> *Think of the love that the Father has lavished on us, by letting us be called God's children; and that is what we are. We are already the children of God but what we are to be in the future has not yet been revealed; all we know is, that when it is revealed we shall be like him because we shall see him as he really is* (1 JN. 3, 1-2).

34   THE FRONT LINE

You are not "just an ordinary layman." For there is nothing ordinary about the layman today. He is not a member of some inferior class of the "many who were called," but not worthy to be among the "few who were chosen."

The time is passed when the laymen can be considered a resigned group of people who take everything on good faith, who go through life with a certain awesome respect for the clergy, and who try to pay their way into God's favor instead of working their way by a dedicated life.

If we think of the layman as ordinary, we risk considering him a member of the Church for his own personal good and not a member of the Church for the good of the Church. Membership in the Church is not a one-way street. It works both ways. The Church must have regard for its members, but the members must also have regard for the Church.

Laymen do not belong to the Church just to get themselves safely into heaven. They have a real stake in the life and work of the Church. They are just as much a vital part of the missionary life of the Church as the clergy.

Pope Pius XII: "The faithful and more precisely the laity are stationed in the front ranks of the life of the Church and through them the Church is the living principle of society. Consequently they especially must have a clearer consciousness not only of belonging to the Church, but of being the Church."

Cardinal Suhard: "The laity have an irreplacable work to do. They have their own witness to bear, their specific problems to solve and reforms to bring about for all of which they are solely responsible."

It is up to each of us to discover our function in the Church. We must search our environment and search ourselves to discover what special gift we can bring to bear, what special contribution we can make to the life of the Church. Human diversity is such a wonderful thing that we need not worry about doing somebody else's job or somebody else doing our job. Each of us has a job to do, a spot to fill. Each is unique. No one else in the world can do it in exactly the same way.

> *If the foot were to say, 'I am not a hand and so I do not belong to the body,' would that mean that it stopped being part of the body? If the ear were to say, 'I am not an eye, and so I do not belong to the body,' would that mean it was not a part of the body? If your whole body were just one eye, how would you hear anything? If it were just one ear, how would you smell anything* (1 COR. 12, 15-17)?

35 OUR WAY OF LIFE

They were seated around the table, Christ and his twelve. Christ had just predicted Peter's denial. Then he added the word of comfort: "and where I go you know, and the way you know." Again it was Thomas who was not willing to take anything at face value. "Lord," he said, "we do not know where you are going, and how can we know the way?" Christ answered without hesitation, "I am the Way. No one comes to the Father except through me."

There is no equivocation here. Christ has made it abundantly clear that there are not many ways, but only one way. All progress in Christian life is to be measured by one norm only — Christ.

We must therefore know Christ. This means we have to make Christ the object of serious study. We have to know the historical Christ, the major events and deeds and teachings of Christ. But more than that we have to know the personality and spirit of Christ. We have to come to know Christ as friend knows friend.

This is not something we will attain merely by study; we have to meditate and contemplate Christ. It is not a sterile, barren knowledge that we seek. But a vibrating, living, vital understanding. Understanding goes deeper than knowledge. There are many people who know us, but very few people who understand us. Understanding is something that goes to the heart. It begets a kindred spirit and community of interest.

The ultimate in understanding comes when we strive to become like the one we are trying to understand. So the third stage in Christian living is imitation. This is how we follow Christ as the Way. By attempting to take on the spirit, the attitude and the motives of Christ, we are following him. We have to strive to make Christ come alive within us.

The chore of the Christian then is threefold — study, understand, imitate Christ. When you break it down like this, it sounds simple. However we must keep in mind that each phase demands concentrated effort. We will have our measure of success and failure. But if we stay with it we will succeed in "putting on the Lord Jesus Christ."

All I want is to know Christ and the power of his resurrection and to share his sufferings by reproducing the pattern of his death (PHIL. 3, 10).

36   GRACE OF WORKING

"We hold that by offering his work to God man becomes associated with the redemptive act itself of Jesus Christ, who conferred an eminent dignity on labor when at Nazareth he worked with his own hands." — Vatican II

St. Francis of Assisi wrote: "Those to whom the Lord has given the grace of working should work faithfully and devotedly in such a way that with idleness the enemy of the soul excluded, they do not extinguish the spirit of holy prayer and devotion to which everything else temporal must give service."

Psychologists tell us that work can satisfy a deep-seated desire of man because it provides a healthy outlet for self-fulfillment. We note how true this is by contrast when we observe the utter demoralizing effect of unemployment. Work can also provide a natural foundation for friendships, loyalties, and the feeling of being needed. These too are basic human wants. Work also engages human energies in wholesome pursuits.

All this sounds so pretty and pious, doesn't it? When the beads of sweat roll down one's brow, when muscle and brain ache under the pressure, when the anxieties mount because someone is breathing down one's neck, all these beautiful platitudes about the dignity of work become so much eyewash. That may be true. All the more reason why we must formulate our philosophy of work in moments of calm.

If we don't get the proper attitude toward work, so much valuable time is wasted, time that could have contributed to one's spiritual growth. The pity is compounded because so much time is spent on a job of some sort. Work and religion do not have to compete. They must not compete. We do not have to take time out from our daily chores to devote to religion. Rather we ought to work in a spirit of "God consciousness," aware in some way that what we do is ordained by the will of God. Our spiritual life must intermesh with our daily work. If it does not, we are short-changing ourselves. If we work it right, the very same job that assures me a paycheck for time can assure me a bonus for eternity. No matter what I do, I can "sacramentalize" it. St. Paul says the same thing: "Whether you eat or drink or whatever else you do, do all for the glory of God."

> Don't delude yourself into thinking God can be cheated: where a man sows, there he reaps: if he sows in the field of self-indulgence, he will get a harvest of corruption out of it; if he sows in the field of the Spirit, he will get from it a harvest of eternal life (GAL. 6, 7-8).

37   A DOSE OF PRAYER

Years ago when the American government took over the Philippine Islands an epidemic was raging. The same epidemic ravaged Japan and India. Strange to say, however, it did not bother China. And stranger still the reason was because the Chinese drink tea. Tea requires boiled water and boiled water kills germs. So the American government told the Filipinos to boil their water. They said they would, but still the epidemic continued.

"Are you boiling your water?"

"Oh, yes."

The officials watched them. They boiled their water all right and then they would take several spoonfuls a day as if it were medicine. But the water they drank and the water they used with their meals was water they had not boiled. Is it any wonder that the epidemic continued?

In our spiritual life, in the supernatural life of the soul we are plagued on all sides by the epidemic of sin and evil. This epidemic continues very often because we take prayer in small doses, sometimes even less than three spoonfuls a day. In order to stay a healthy Christian a little dab of prayer won't do. We have to drink long and deep at the fount of prayer.

No matter what book you pick up on the spiritual life, you will always find a treatise on prayer. It is treated often and in great length because prayer is important. If a person does not pray his salvation is in jeopardy. And spoonful prayer will not suffice. Our life has to be saturated with prayer. So very much depends upon it.

If we pray well, we live well. If we live well, we die well. If we die well, all is well.

It goes back to our prayer life. If a person perseveres in prayer, he cannot but improve his life. First of all because prayer is a source of grace. Second, the natural psychology of the act. If you raise your mind and heart to God, speak to God on intimate terms one of two things will happen, either you will want to make yourself worthy to speak with God and thus do the necessary violence to self to accomplish this. Or you will stop praying, or your praying will be reduced to the mechanical recital of some set formula which is tantamount to not praying.

So if we pray well, we live well; if we live well, we die well; if we die well, all is well.

But the hour will come — in fact it is here already — when true worshippers will worship the Father in spirit and truth: that is the kind of worshipper the Father wants (JN. 4, 23).

38   STAY FIT*

He knew it. He just knew that one day his big chance would come. He was dying to show everybody what a good tackle he was. So far this season there was nothing spectacular. But now they found themselves confronted with the game for the championship. Half a minute left in the game. His team was winning by a slim one point. The opposing halfback broke into the clear. Only he stood between the runner and a TD. This was the chance of a lifetime. His chance to be a hero. He filled his lungs, stretched his legs, gave it all he had. It wasn't enough. His lungs ached; his legs became leaden. The halfback outran him. A championship within reach, but he did not have what it takes. In the locker room nobody looked at him. They knew. Only the coach did not know that the reason why he failed was because he was out of condition. All season he thought himself above training rules. Everybody knew he had been breaking training all season. Just a small beer here, later hours occasionally, a short smoke. Nothing serious. But when the big test came, he did not have what it takes because he had broken training.

Life is like that. We have to keep in training. The prize is not merely a championship. The prize is eternity. And I must keep in training for eternity. Of course it is easy to sin just a "little here and a little there." Nothing really big. But if I get out of training on these little matters, will I have what I need when the big matter comes along? Every life has the big test, the serious temptation to sin. We will be no match unless we keep in training.

The training rules are there. We know them well. There is no coach looking over our shoulder. We are on our own. To get away with something is as easy as pie. No one may ever find out. But when the big chance comes, we will know why we did not have what it takes.

St. Paul had the right word for it: "But I chastise my body and bring it into subjection, lest perhaps after preaching to others I myself should be rejected."

---

*See *Mental Prayer*, Queen's Work.

> *There is no necessity for us to obey our unspiritual selves or to live unspiritual lifes. If you do live in that way, you are doomed to die; but if by the spirit you put an end to the misdeeds of the body, you will live* (ROM. 8, 12-13).

39   CRISIS IN CHANGE

Everywhere we turn people are nervous. They are anxious, unsure, unsettled. World events are turning topsy-turvy. Our sense of security is jarred. Up to now we had the consolation that, come what may, at least the Church is stable. Here we have a haven of peace, a sense of unchanging eternity.

But now people are wondering even about that. Look at all the changes that are taking place. Not even the Mass is untouched. Of all things, we thought that was untouchable. Give the "litniks" their way and so many traditions fall by the wayside. Something seems to be happening to our safe anchors.

The changes are shattering some of our ideals. This is what people are saying. Witness for example the remark of the young school teacher who had just entered an invalid marriage. "Why worry? In a few years the Church will approve of even this union."

No one can doubt that we are passing through a transition and transitions are always unsettling and difficult times. We don't doubt there will be many tragedies and defections before the changes are completed. It need not be so, however, if we recognize that from the very beginning the Church is a mystery, a reality imbued with a Divine Presence and for that reason susceptible of new and deeper investigation. The Vatican Council was engaged in such an investigation. The Council's intent was to penetrate this mystery deeper and deeper. To force us to think with her, Mother Church has nudged us in an area that touches us directly, the liturgy. This is the Church's immediate contact with her people. Since the changes began, people are talking about the Church. This is good. The talk may be tainted with anxiety but it is also colored with love and confidence. All we need is more time.

An awareness of our involvement with the Church strikes us with a jarring jolt, like the realization that knocked Paul from his horse. The Holy Spirit operates in unlikely ways. This awareness must precede the renewal of spirit toward which the Church is working. When this renewal is accomplished, the Church can then show herself to the world without apology and declare: "Who sees me, sees Christ." Until then we have to refrain from precipitous action and give the Holy Spirit just a little more time.

All I can say is that I forget the past and I strain ahead for what is still to come I am racing for the finish, for the prize to which God calls us upwards to receive in Christ Jesus (PHIL. 3, 14-15).

40 SOURCE OF GRACE

Man is endowed with some wonderful powers of body and mind. He is able to force open the closed fist of nature and make her reveal her marvels. His ingenuity has contrived some very clever and very awesome inventions. With all his power and cleverness, however, man of himself cannot rise to the supernatural level for which he was created. For this the hand of God himself must reach down from the heights of heaven and lift him up. It is in the Mass that we get in touch with God because from the Mass we get grace.

The Mass is one of the chief means of grace because of its unique relation with the sacrifice of Calvary. Calvary is the primary source of all grace. It is the fountainhead of the graces and blessings of redemption. By his death on the cross Christ restored the supernatural order of grace. It is to the redeeming blood of Christ that we owe every grace accruing from all the sacraments. There is attached, we might say, a drop of the precious blood of Christ.

Since the sacrifice of the Mass and the sacrifice of Calvary are so intimately related, the fruit of each is likewise intimately related. The fruit of Calvary is grace. The fruit of the Mass is grace. This is the difference. On the cross grace was earned; grace was merited. On the altar grace is distributed; grace is handed out.

If we realize that grace is God's contact with man; if we understand that grace elevates man to God's level, we will begin to appreciate the value of the Mass. All the ambitious devices that science can invent, all the marvelous achievements of man's wisdom, all the awe-inspiring powers of nature can never achieve what one Mass can accomplish. The pity is that so few understand this and as a result morning after morning the Mass is offered before empty pews. To be sure there is some sacrifice entailed in getting to Mass. But the price is so meager and the prize so great.

Whether the sacrifice of the Mass is offered in pontifical splendor in some magnificent cathedral or in humble simplicity in some missionary's hut, the Mass will always be the one supreme Catholic sacrifice. It will always remain the throbbing heart of the Mystical Body pumping life-giving grace to all the members of that Mystical Body.

> *How much more effectively the blood of Christ, who offered himself as the perfect sacrifice to God through the eternal Spirit, can purify our inner self from dead actions so that we do our service to the living God* (HEB. 9, 14).

41   ESSENCE OF LIFE

"Do I really love God?" Have you ever asked yourself that question with the creeping anxiety that perhaps you did not love him? How does a person know?

In trying to answer that important question there is danger in thinking of love of God in terms of affection. We imagine we do not love God because there is no special thrill in getting out of bed Sunday morning and rushing to Mass. Or we do not find ourselves tapping our foot, anxious for the party to break up, so we can get to our prayers. I'm sure that most of us feel greater affection toward some particular person than we do toward God.

If you have ever been in love, there is no doubt that you experienced some very strong feelings toward the person you love, feelings which arose spontaneously. They were not something you could crank up at will. They were there or they were not there, pretty much beyond your control.

Because we have this kind of experience in human love, we think that when we are commanded to love God there has to be a quickening of the pulse, excitement of the emotions, and all the other physical reflexes. This is the mistake we make. If these reactions are not there, we scold ourselves for not loving God. The fact of the matter is we need not work ourselves up to an emotional lather. There need be no feeling or emotion at all. They may be there. If they are, fine. That is a bonus. But if they are not there, this is no reason for concern, because we are not expected to love God with an emotional love. This is evident from the fact that we are commnaded to love God. An emotion cannot be commanded. So there must be some other way to love God.

There is. We are expected to love him with a deliberate love. This is a choosing, a cold calculating preference whereby we give God priority in our lives and especially when we don't feel like doing it. It is an act of the will that puts God before everything else, even our feelings.

This may seem odd to us who are accustomed to live by feeling. Nevertheless it is something we have to learn to accept if we want to understand how to love God. This preference of God must be made with our whole heart, not only with what is left over after we have loved everything else. With our whole soul, not only the part that hopes to get to heaven. With our whole mind, not only if we have room left over after our pursuit of worldly knowledge. Loving God to the fulness of our ability is the essence of Christian living.

> God is love and anyone who lives in love lives in God,
> and God lives in him (1 JN. 4, 16).

42　NOW

"Do you need money? All it takes is one phone call. Let us help you. No red tape; no fuss. Signature is all we need. Convenient monthly payments. Low interest rates." This is the tempting offer heard frequently on radio and TV. When bills are due and creditors are breathing down one's neck, this can be a very alluring offer. Many people fall for it to their regret.

It sounds so good beforehand but after you get your money it is a different story. Those low monthly charges eat cancerously into an already small income. In a very real way the lifeblood of the family is drained. It is said that one in thirty-three of the civil service workers in an eastern city has his salary garnisheed by loan sharks. This story is repeated throughout the country. Millions of people — farmers, day laborers, teachers, small business men — all have fallen prey to the unscrupulous "loan sharks" with their "juice men" to enforce payment. The unwary are easily trapped. Indiscriminate borrowing of money can be dangerous.

Indiscriminate borrowing of money may be dangerous but indiscriminate borrowing on our time may be more dangerous and disastrous. "When I get time, I'll get back to God. I'm having too much fun now. I'll work on that bad habit tomorrow. Too busy now. Later. There is still plenty of time." Delayed reform is borrowing on time.

The unfortunate point is that such borrowed tomorrows are payments we never meet. Borrowing on time today to be paid up tomorrow will bankrupt our future life. Every passing day that we put off doing something we know we should do is allowing the devil to garnishee our life. By and by leads to neverland.

But there is a limit. We come to the end of the line when "death," that "juice man of life" forces the payment. Those little shreds of time that we borrowed so blissfully now have to be paid back in terms of eternity and the interest rate is exorbitant.

It is too late then to harbor regrets for not having husbanded our time and resources better. When the squeeze is on, it is too late to resolve to make better use of the present moment. It is too late when time runs out. "Now is the acceptable time. Let us work while there is still light." Using our time well is like putting money in the bank. Then we will have the coin that passes for legal tender in the life to come.

Stay awake, because you do not know the day when your master is coming. You may be quite sure of this that if the householder had known at what time of the night the burglar would come, he would have stayed

> *awake and would not have allowed anyone to break*
> *through the wall of his house. Therefore, you too must*
> *stand ready because the Son of Man is coming at an*
> *hour you do not expect* (MT. 24, 42-44).

43   ST. FRANCIS

St. Francis was a little man with a big heart who made such a success of this business of living because he was so much like his master.

St. Francis was a "little man," that is he was humble. The fact that people thronged after him he explained this way: "That is happening to me because of the eyes of God on high taking in everywhere the good and the bad. Those most holy eyes have espied nobody among the sinners more useless, incompetent and sinful than me and to do the marvels he has in mind, he has found no more worthless creature on earth. And so he has choosen me to put to shame what is noble and grand and powerful and fair and wise about the world, so that it may be clear that all virtue and all that is good comes from him and not from any creature; and no person may glory in his sight, but whoever glories shall glory in the Lord, to whom be all honor and glory forever.

The great secret of Francis' humility was this: he thought and acted and lived as if no one existed on earth but God and himself. He was so overwhelmed by the power and perfection of God that everything else paled into insignificance, himself included.

Francis had a "big heart." He was charitable, generous, all-embracing in his love. By nature he was warm and affectionate. He was a born lover. To love great things and to be great in love had always been the need of his heart. His whole heart and soul vibrated with seraphic love of God and man. For the sake of this love he would relinquish his right to life of comfort and ease. For the sake of this love he would give of himself without stint. No matter how much he did, he was not satisfied. In the last days of his life he said, "Let us now begin for up to now we have done nothing." His heart was too big for his frail body which all too soon gave up.

Francis was "so much like his Master." He was like a man walking in a circle and at the center of that circle was Christ. He strove to live and work for truth as Christ did. He hated sham and hypocrisy as Christ hated them. He sought to acquire some of the patience and kindness, the love and tolerance, the understanding and gentleness of Christ. He sought to merge his personality with the personality of Christ. So well did he succeed that heaven itself put the visible stamp of approval on his hand and feet and side.

> As for me the only thing I can boast about is the cross of our Lord Jesus Christ, through whom the world is crucified to me and I to the world. The marks on my body are those of Jesus (GAL. 6, 14-17b).

44 LIVE COALS

There is no substitute for a well-developed interior, spiritual life. Without this we are smoke without fire, a flickering flame without heat.

Without a deeply spiritual life we are like the janitor of a poor country church. He loathed the very idea of getting up on cold wintry mornings to build a fire in the big pot-bellied stove. The parishioners complained without letup. Finally the pastor said: do your job or else. The following Sunday there were no complaints because the flickering flame visible through the cracks appeased the critical congregation. But the pastor still felt the chill. After services he investigated. He opened the stove door and found, instead of burning logs, two burning candles. The flickering flame was there but there was no heat.

Do we not have a repetition of this incident in the life of the Christian who is satisfied with mere external activities? He may succeed in fooling the people with the flicker of feigned devotion but Christ still feels the chill. And Christ has some strong words for these people: "I would that you were hot or cold, but because you are lukewarm and neither hot nor cold, I am about to vomit you out of my mouth."

Let's face it. Anything external that the Christian engages in can be duplicated by the pagan and in many instances with greater effectiveness. They can fight poverty, they can take care of the needy, they can counsel the neurotic. They have their breadlines, their halfway houses, their rehabilitation centers. There must be something to distinguish the Christian who does parallel work.

That something is a cultivation of deep spiritual life.

If we do not have that, we are traveling under false colors. We are not loyal to our calling. Now don't misunderstand me, the active life has its place in the plan of God. Since Vatican II we have a serious obligation to get deeply involved with the world. It seems to me to be a lot of waste of energy unless this involvement is activated by the dynamo of the interior spiritual life.

Years ago when Hugh Benson toured America he was asked what his impression was of American Christian life. He replied: "In America there is too much Martha and not enough Mary." Can it be that we are still busy about many things but neglectful of the most important one?

> *Fill your minds with everything that is true, everything that is noble, everything that is good and pure, everything that we love and honor, and everything that can be thought virtuous or worthy of praise* (PHIL. 4, 8).

45 'TIS THE SEASON

Feelings run high at Christmas time. Instinctively we all look upon Christmas as a special day for children and children are mostly creatures of feeling. Feelings are good. They are part of our human body-soul equipment. Without feelings we would be strange indeed.

As we get more mature, however, we learn to temper our feelings and try to root them firmly in convictions. Our feelings at Christmas then must be based on the firm conviction that the Christ Child is the Son of God. In him there is a unique union of the human and divine in such a way that the human does not lessen the divine and the divine does not absorb the human.

With this in mind there are several sound feelings we ought to elicit at Christmas:

Let us be grateful. When we recall what a tremendous favor God has bestowed on us at the first Christmas, can we be anything but grateful? Almighty God, who in the beginning has given human nature so much, ennobled that same human nature by sharing it with us. In sharing it with us he has brought a fuller life endowing us with the seeds of eternity.

Let us be sympathetic. Christ was not born in the air-conditioned convenience of the 20th century. The very necessities of life were in scarce supply. As we reconstruct that first Christmas night, let's take note that Christ embraced privation and suffering. This was a prelude to the life he was to live for us. Surely our hearts will go out in sympathy.

Let us be contrite. Maybe this is a sour note in the joyful harmony of Christmas, but we dare not overlook the fact that the circumstances of Christ's birth were in some way connected with the sin of man — our sin. Inasmuch as we have contributed to the sinfulness of the human race, we should have a feeling of contrition. We maintain the proper perspective when we keep this in mind.

With the jingling of bells and the crackle of wrapping paper, we must always bear in mind the deeper meaning of Christmas.

Parish Bulletin, Liguorian Press.

46   A LAYMAN'S NEED*

There is a great deal of talk today about spirituality and sanctity for the layman. More and more people are writing about the subject but some of them are watering down the valid notion of sanctity until it has become a caricature. Any spirituality for the laymen, regardless what particular brand a person may pursue, must have certain essential qualities to warrant the title.

First of all the layman must have an interior and personal discipline. Since he, by definition, does not join a community he must discipline his own life with the spirit of the Gospels. This cannot be a spread-shot effort. So some kind of system tailored to his peculiar needs and capabilities is needed.

Second, the layman must sanctify himself in and through the temporal. Since he lives in the world, he must utilize the world in achieving sanctity. This is a reversal of the attitude that would flee from the world. The fact is the layman must step into heaven from his office, his classroom, his workbench, his kitchen.

Third, not only must he strive to practice justice, fortitude, temperance, and prudence, but also related virtues like sincerity, loyalty, kindness, simplicity. In other words the so-called natural virtues.

Fourth, in the apostolic work which is being urged upon the layman on all sides, it is imperative that he combine action with prayer or contemplation. He must dare to do, but at the same time he must not forget his own inadequacies. It is this abiding sense of inadequacies that forces him to rely on contemplation.

Finally, the person in the world must practice a type of asceticism that is best suited for himself. Each of us has his own abilities and limitations. Each one then must determine for himself what his capacity is. This means an honest appraisal — not too high and not too low.

We keep returning to this notion of sanctity for the laity because it is an important subject. But we can't help wondering if our people really understand its value.

---

*Adapted from Joseph Folliet.

47 BEACON LIGHT

To hear some people talk you would imagine that they see over the archway of life what Dante saw over the archway to hell: "Abandon all hope you who enter here." The moment an American is born he begins to owe the U. S. government several thousand dollars. Our days are trying days with death and destruction, want and sickness, wars and rumors of wars, hot and cold. It would seem that the hand of God is resting heavily on this world.

Throughout this maelstrom, like a beacon beckoning us to a resurgence of life, stands the virtue of hope. There is something eternally young about hope. It puts a spring in our step and lilt in our voice. Life, after all, need not be a dull plodding affair. It is a swift action, rushing to an end that is worthy of our freedom. It is hope that gives buoyancy to our strivings because hope gives us the assurance of the means to that goal.

Hope holds tenaciously to the reasonable middle between the two unreasonable extremes of presumption and despair. The despairing soul sees no remedy and the presumptuous soul needs no remedy. The one gives up the search for heaven and the other gives up the avoidance of hell. Hope walks the thin golden thread in the middle. Hope relying on the omnipotent mercy of God avoids despair. Hope stressing the omnipotent justice of God avoids presumption.

Hope must be built up by all the means at our disposal. The ideal place is in the home. To achieve this parents can stress the motives on which hope is founded, the infinite power of God and his boundless mercy. We must live with the realization that God has the power and the will to help us. This means turning to God daily in the trials and toils, the joys and accomplishments of life. Too often God is looked to as the last resort when all other means have been exhausted, whereas he ought to be the first resource to which we turn. By turning to God first, parents create an atmosphere in which children are imbued with the basis of firm hope.

We don't doubt the mercy of God, but do we allow this truth to absorb our being? Absorb our being it must, but in an enlightened way. God is infinitely powerful and merciful. However, he is not fondly foolish. He will never squander his graces nor sow them at random on barren soil. Our hope therefore must be reasonable lest we set our sights on something for which we have no right to hope.

> *For we must be content to hope that we shall be saved — our salvation is not in sight, we should not have to be hoping for it if it were — but, as I say, we must hope to be saved since we are not saved yet — it is something we must wait for with patience* (ROM. 8, 24-25).

48   SURE-FIRE FORMULA

No sooner do we awake to consciousness when we feel the world pressing upon us from a hundred sides. At first we are puzzled, then intrigued and finally obsessed with the world and the things of the world. These exert a strange relentless fascination over us. They entwine themselves around our heart and worm their way into our pattern of thinking and living so much so that what was intended by God to be a helpmate becomes a domineering tyrant. The pity is that our judgment can become so warped that we often prefer the creatures of God to the God of creatures. We call this the greed of possession.

Second, God has chosen to share his creative power with his creatures. Sometimes he asks for the use of this faculty and sometimes he asks for the sacrifice of it. If kept within the realm of faith, conscience, and reason there is nothing so sublime as the power of procreation. Unfortunately, since the fall of man, this power has a tendency of getting out of hand. In its grosser forms it reveals itself in sex aberrations. In its more refined forms, it is manifested in undue pampering of the body. When whims, fancies, and demands of the flesh take precedence over duty and obligation, we call it the lust for pleasure.

Third, it does not take shrewd observation to notice that man is prone to insist on his own way in everything. He plots and counterplots just to have things his way. He will brook no opposition. Somehow he develops the attitude that his side of the question is always the right side. I think the best way to describe this person is to compare him with an egg. An egg is so full of itself that there is no room for anything else. So too a person who makes no effort to curb his self-will is so full of himself that there is little room for anything else; sometimes there is no room even for God himself. This is pride of power.

These three, the greed of possession, the lust for pleasure, and the pride of power are the fundamental obstacles we have to hurdle if we want to grow in our love of God. Obviously, a life cannot be God-centered if it is worldly-minded, pleasure-bound, and self-willed. If we want to get closer to God, we have to combat the greed of possession by the spirit of detachment; the lust for pleasure by the spirit of mortification; and the pride of power by humility and obedience.

> *If your right eye should cause you to sin, tear it out and throw it away; for it will do you less harm to lose one part of you than to have your whole body thrown into hell* (MT. 5, 29).

49   GOODNESS GRACIOUS

Goodness in action is love. Daily we experience the goodness of God in action. But how many of us see clearly that it is the loving hand of God that is gently dispensing his goodness.

If we are sensitive, we can see God's goodness in the experience of a truly good man. In every life there are those who walk with us for awhile and we are the better for their goodness, kindness, and understanding. They come to us in need, give us of their own riches. When they leave, something wonderful remains behind.

The man who helps a stalled motorist, the little girl who guides a blind grandfather, the gent who directs the bewildered traveler who has lost his way — these are good people who reflect the goodness of God.

We see God's goodness also in his loving pursuit of us. Francis Thompson in his *Hound of Heaven* graphically portrays the soul of every man in his frenzied search for substitutes for God. In the end the taste is bitter and empty.

It is through God's insistent goodness that we come to know him who truly loves us. Scripture tells us that even when we were in sin, God loved us. Calvary proves it. It is this pursuing love of God that is perhaps the most disarming experience of his goodness.

A realization of the goodness of God is the starting point for our spiritual life. Once we realize this, we sense the need of preparing ourselves to mirror this goodness to others. This we do by developing as thoroughly as possible our talents and abilities, by using our time and opportunities to further the kingdom of God.

We must strive to have within us "the spirit of the Lord and his holy operation." We are to surrender ourselves completely to the transforming grace of God and be alert to the inspiration to become real instruments of his will. We are to die to self in order to be free from sin, to curb passions and unsavory tendencies of greed, lust, and power.

Once this groundwork is laid, or even in the process of laying this groundwork, we must reach out to others. We must respond to the blind, the maimed, the sick, the weak, the elderly, the handicapped. Goodness in action — this is Christianity, for this is love.

> *Out of his infinite glory, may he give you the power through his spirit for your hidden self to grow strong, so that Christ may live in your hearts through faith, and then, planted in his love and built on love, you will with all the saints have strength to grasp the breadth and the length, the height and the depth, until knowing the love of Christ, which is beyond all knowledge, you are filled with the utter fulness of God* (EPH. 3, 16-19).

50   UP-TO-DATE

"So we have made some changes. Big deal. You have me standing more than I care to, you have me sitting on cue, you have me croaking in my off-tune voice. So what? I don't feel any holier. In fact I resent the whole matter because it interferes with my prayer life. It is a big distraction to me."

Why couldn't they leave well enough alone? Because it was not "well enough." Imperceptibly the matter had gotten out of kilter. What seems to have happened is what happens when the picture and sound of a movie are not synchronized. The direct communication is impeded. We have to strain to get the message. So with the Mass. The rite itself, because of altered conditions, no longer spoke directly to us. We needed someone to intervene — a translator or a missal or commentator or extraneous reading matter. What the Church is attempting to do now is to synchronize picture and sound, rite and message, so that we get the communication directly.

But even this is not the main point. What the Church is searching for is relevancy. How can the saving, sanctifying purpose of the Church be fitted to the actual needs of the people of our times. What she is striving for is to update her approach so that her message will be more meaningful to modern man. Ultimately she is trying to renew the inner man, the spirit. Through the liturgy, which is only one avenue of encounter, the Church is trying to reawaken a sense of Christian commitment. She is looking for conversion, a change of heart. She is trying to shape our attitudes so we become effective instruments in fulfilling our mission of carrying to all the world the love and truth and power of Christ.

This will not come about automatically. Certainly a mere change in the liturgy is not going to produce the desired effects. There has to be good will. Each of us must make the effort to study, to ponder, to meditate the whole matter. We have to feel the new vitality surging through the Church and realize that we are part of it. We have to become absorbed in the life of the Church, and understand that this struggle for relevancy is also our struggle for we are the Church.

> *So you are no longer aliens or foreign visitors: you are citizens like all the saints, and part of God's household. You are a part of the building that has the apostles and prophets for its foundations, and Christ Jesus himself for its main cornerstone* (EPH. 2, 19-20).

51 THE LOWEST HEIGHT

One day an old Irish grandmother took her four-year-old grandson with her to evening services. She pointed out the various objects in church and explained each item — the holy water font, the communion rail, the altar, the pulpit and so on.

She then told him that in the tabernacle was Christ himself. There was a brief silence; then the lad said, "Granma, Christ is God, isn't he?" "Yes, Christ is God." Another silence ensued. "God is big, isn't he? Real big?" "Yes." A longer silence. Finally the lad blurted out, "If God is so big, why does he live in that little house on the altar?"

Here is a child trying to solve the mystery of Christ's humility in the Blessed Sacrament. Why Christ should so humble himself in the Eucharist, will always be hard for us to understand. But the fact is there. There is no denying that.

It all began back on the first Christmas night. On that memorable night Christ stooped from the highest heights of heaven to earth from divinity to humanity. A God became man. That was the profoundest humility.

St. Paul writes: "He emptied himself taking the form of a slave." But that wasn't the end. He went even further in his humiliation. Consider the scourging at the pillar, the crowning with thorns, the ridicule of the mob, the crucifixion between two thieves. The words of Jeremias come to mind, "I am a worm and no man."

In the crib and on the cross Christ still retains the outer form of a man. That in itself was some dignity, not at all approaching the dignity of a God-man but still some dignity.

There is, however, a more profound and deeper depth to which Christ would lower himself. On our altars he emptied himself even of his outer form of a man. He took upon himself the form of ground wheat and crushed grape. He is present under the veil of bread and wine.

In all these acts of lowering himself, Christ manifests something that is very important in humility — total dependence on the will of his heavenly Father. That is the essence of humility, a declaration of dependence.

Humility is to acknowledge the truth about ourselves. And the truth about ourselves is that we are totally dependent upon God for everything we have and everything we are.

Once we recognize that we are completely dependent on God and act on this truth, everything else falls into place. We see the hand of God in all the good we do, we see the hand of God in all the talents we possess, we see the hand of God hovering over us in benediction.

> *Remember how generous the Lord Jesus was: he was rich, but he became poor for your sake, to make you rich out of his poverty* (2 COR. 8, 9).

52 HELP WANTED

The Chairman of the Board of DuPont, Crawford Greenealt, said: "The capacity for creative accomplishment is a precious commodity, not to be wasted, not to be diluted. We need great ability throughout the entire nation. We must have able men in the government, able men in business, able men in the professions, our full share of creative output in literature and in the arts, no less than we need all of these things in science . . . The society that creates scientists by diminishing the ranks of its philosophers may in the end have little need for either."

When God made the world he could have finished it, but he didn't. He left it as a raw material, to tease us, to tantalize us, to set us thinking and experimenting and risking and adventuring. This engenders a supreme interest in living.

Have you ever noticed that small children will often ignore the clever mechanical toys in order to build, with spool and string and sticks and blocks, a world of their own imagination? And so with grown-ups.

God gave us a world unfinished so we might share in the joy and satisfaction of creation. He left electricity in the clouds. He left diamonds uncut. He gave us the challenge of raw materials, not the satisfaction of perfect, finished things. He left music unsung and drama unplayed. He left poetry undreamed in order that men and women might not become bored but engaged in exciting, stimulating creative activities that keep them thinking, working, experimenting and experiencing all the joys and lasting satisfaction of achievement.

There is no Shangri-La where every wish and whim is supplied. There is nothing worth while gained by chance. Work, thought, creation — these give life its stimulus, its real satisfaction, its intriguing value.

Look around you. Look within you. Discover your potential. Discover your opportunity. There are still mountains to scale, songs to be sung, poems to be dreamed. Our forebears have not exhausted the possibilities. There is room in every area for the person who is willing to pay the price.

53   A SECOND LOOK

"You can't say 'no' all the time." This was the answer the mother gave, grasping for an excuse, no matter how feeble. She was tired of disappointing her child. That was her only reason for giving permission this time. Perhaps it did not occur to her (whose daughter was killed in a night auto accident) that she would not have to say "no" continually if a code said "no" for her. If the baby asks for matches, there is no pussy-footing around. Matches mean fire, and fire destroys life. Underlying our refusal is a definite code. That dictates the reply.

Unfortunately too many parents make up their rules from day to day, and often fancy and mood determine the issue. Among other things this reveals a sad lack of prudence, which is a frequent cause of friction between parents and children. The correct answer to moral problems is not always the most appealing because our darkened intellect and weakened will are formidable obstacles.

Prudence, however, helps us to choose the adequate means to accomplish what God wants us to do. In more complicated issues prudence demands that we investigate by study and consultation. It helps too to recall past judgments in similar situations. In this manner we are more sure of pointing in the right direction. Once the decision is made, sentimentality must not be allowed to get the upper hand. Prudence in parents is more apt to win the love and respect of children. Once they are convinced of prudent counsel and advice, they are less likely to shun it.

Prudence is the virtue of the strong and resolute and its earnestness will command respect and compliance in those critical hours when a child's confidence in his parent is hanging in balance. Prudence will dictate punishment when necessary but it will always guide the hand lest the punishment exceed due measure. At times prudence must be stern and severe but at all times it must be sympathetic and understanding.

Prudence is not taught in a book; it is caught from God. It is a gift we pray for and in a day when so much depends on the guidance parents give, prudence must be high on our list of requests.

54   NO SMALL MATTER

As I crossed the great Mississippi River, I could not but be impressed. It commanded respect from the entire surrounding area. Men had to build immense bridges to cross it. Homes had to keep a healthy distance. Huge barges were carried along effortlessly and its depths were teeming with life. Yet, if you trace the mighty Mississippi to its origin, you discover that it begins in an unimpressive manner. A little trickle from a mountain stream converges with numerous rivulets which together swell in volume as they make their way to the gulf. None of these little streams in themselves attract notice, but one cannot but admire the strength, the beauty, and the might of the majestic river.

This is how sanctity builds up. Sanctity is not a prefab job. We are not handed halos at birth. It starts with a drop of God's grace. This grace used properly calls forth other graces. Each time we use a grace we build up a stream of growing sanctity, until we have the mighty river of sanctifying grace sweeping everything before it. But remember it all started small.

> "All life is made of small things
> Little leaves make up the trees
> And many tiny drops of water
> Blending make the mighty seas."

No one, certainly none of the saints, is catapulted into holiness. It is not a matter of pressing an elevator button and being carried to cloud No. 9. It is more a matter like walking up a flight of stairs. We have to take one step at a time, dragging one foot after the other. It is the little, seemingly insignificant things of life, that make up our sanctity.

This calls for fidelity to the grace of the moment. If we use that well, we get the next. Judged by this standard there are no insignificant events in our lives. Each event has a bearing on our growth in sanctity.

> *His master said to him, "Well done, good and faithful servant; you have shown you can be faithful in small things, I will trust you with greater; come and join your master's happiness"* (MT. 25, 23).

55 HEART AND SOUL

The two children were so excited they could hardly open the monastery door. They were so breathless they could scarcely stammer: "It's gone, Father, it's gone!"

"What's gone?"

"Somebody stole it!"

"Stole what?"

"The Christ Child from the crib in the monastery yard."

Sure enough. There it stood. Everything in its place; everything pointing to the manager, but the Christ Child was missing. A Christmas crib without a Christ Child struck terror in the hearts of these children. Christmas would not be Christmas without a Christ Child. Oh, for the wisdom of children! They have a way of getting to the heart of a matter.

Now we are not going to ask you to join a crusade to "put Christ back into Christmas." We are not going to ask you to discard our traditional Christmas customs. We are simply asking you to reconsider. Let's not become so engrossed in doing the customary things that we forget why we do them. Many of our customs originally had a connection with Christ and his birth and there is no harm in retaining them as long as their origin in Christ is remembered.

For instance, Christmas gift-giving is meant to be an expression of love. Its purpose is to remind us of the great Gift of Love on the first Christmas night. Our decorations and delicacies indicate a festive spirit, that inner joy we feel because Christ came into this bleak and dark world bringing light. Our special regard for the poor at Christmas time is inspired by the poverty of Christ. In the back of our mind we link the poor with Christ who identified himself with them. Even Santa Claus as an intermediary in giving gifts does not detract from the true meaning of Christmas especially if we recall that St. Nicholas was one of the saints who practiced the charity of Christ.

It is not so much that we have to throw overboard our Christmas customs. They do not necessarily need changing. What does need changing is the attitude of the people who follow these customs but have forgotten the meaning behind them.

If then, we want a norm to determine how much of Christ is in our Christmas, just ask ourselves the question: "Why?" Why are we sending cards? Why are we giving gifts? Why are we helping the poor? Why are we singing carols?

> *The Word was made flesh, he lived among us, and we saw his glory, the glory that is his as the only Son of the Father, full of grace and truth* (JN. 1, 14).

56   LOVE-IN

Love makes the world go round. This is true literally. It is by love that we are made ànd it is for love that we are made. Because God is love, we have come into existence. Because God is love, we exist for love because we exist for God.

Throughout our entire life our attention centers on love. In the name of love and for the sake of love we work, struggle, suffer. Our history is an unending reaction to love, satisfied when it is there, hurt when it is absent. The most deep-seated yearning of the human heart is "love me."

Why all this concern about love? Because we are a reflection of our Creator. I believe this concern about love is really an often unexpressed and many times an unknown desire to approach God. It does not always come on so well because somewhere along the line a distortion has set in. It is like standing before one of those trick mirrors in the amusement park that twists and misshapes our image. What we see is not the real item but a caricature. As our life unfolds, we find ourselves fixing our gaze on material possessions, on sensual pleasure, on our own sweet will, little realizing that we are playing tricks on ourselves. The true object of our love is twisted and distorted. We think we love possessions, pleasure and our own way of doing things, but in the end find little personal fulfillment.

Pleasures, possessions, and pride are thère. There is no denying them. However, if we view these things in the proper perspective, the true goal of our strivings emerges. To maintain the proper perspective requires a determined effort not to allow material possessions to worm their way into our way of living that they become insurmountable obstacles. It means putting a check on our desire for pleasure because man is more than flesh and nerve. It means striving to make our will square with the will of our Creator.

To the extent that we rein in these lesser loves, we are free to experience true Love of our life and feel truly loved. This is the experience that gives fulfillment and a lasting meaning to life.

As long as we respond to the distorted images of the trick mirrors, we will walk away from our purpose of life. In that measure our life will be frustrated, confused, empty. It takes courage to close our ears to the siren call and close our eyes to the glittering dazzle, but this is the price of love. There can be no true love without sacrifice.

Love does make the world go round. But we have to distinguish carefully the kind of love we have in mind.

> *Nothing therefore can come between us and the love of Christ, even if we are troubled or worried, or being persecuted, or lacking food or clothes, or being threatened or even attacked* (ROM. 8, 35).

57   CHRISTIFY ONESELF

The emphasis has shifted. Formerly if anyone wanted to get serious about the business of sanctifying and saving his soul, he was strongly urged to leave the world and flee its contagion. There is still a need to flee the contagion of the world, but Vatican II has added something new. "Each individual layman must stand before the world as a witness to the resurrection and life of the Lord Jesus and a symbol of the living God."

In a very real way the world has a claim on us. Pope Paul wrote: "The Church looks at the world with profound understanding, with sincere admiration and with sincere intention not of conquering it, but of serving it; not of despising it, but of appreciating it; not of condemning it, but of strengthening and saving it."

Where does the Church have its broadest contact with the world? In its members, especially the laymen. The objective of the Church then can be attained best through the layman whose life is intermeshed with the modern world and who understands the sensibilities of modern man. To accomplish this task the layman must work in and through the world. At the same time he must find a way to avoid defilement while working in and through the world.

He must, first of all, get a clear and definite concept of the kind of person he wants to be. He does well to look to Christ who came not only to die for us but to show us how to live in the teeming bustle of humanity. Striving for perfection and excellence in the spirit of Christ is an ideal worthy of serious consideration. St. Paul reminds us that we are called to the "mature measure of the fulness of Christ."

There is talk today about lay spirituality, as if it were some kind of new commodity. The essence still is Christ. This does not change and the layman is going to be able to pull his weight only to the extent that Christ comes alive in his life. In the final analysis it is an individual effort with the individual acting in the context of all his various associations, rarely in isolation. Normally it is impossible to divorce oneself from the community, small and fragmented though it be. This means that the modern man must christify himself in the modern world with modern means. The key word remains the same in every generation — christify. There may be variations and emphases. These by and large are peripheral; the core is Christ, the complete Christ incarnated in every man of good will and vitally concerned about all the ambitions, aspirations, and interests of the "images of God" who people the earth.

> *You must give up your old way of life; you must put aside your old self, which gets corrupted by following illusory desires. Your mind must be renewed by a spiritual revolution so that you can put on the new self that has been created in God's way, in the goodness and holiness of truth* (EPH. 4, 22-23).

58   LOVE OF COUNTRY

From the headquarters of the French army came the order: no one is allowed to attend Mass. This was a Masonic attempt to undermine the faith of the Catholic soldiers. One morning the general accosted a captain with the rebuke: "Captain Foch, it is reported that men under your command are attending Mass. Who are they?"

"I don't know," replied the captain, "I always occupy the front pew and I do not turn around to see who is present."

In spite of orders from higher up, Captain Foch was rendering to God the things that belonged to God. By that same gesture, he was rendering to Caesar the things that belong to Caesar, because as history proved, he was one of the great patriots of France.

The best citizen, the best patriot, is the one who renders to God the things that are God's. By obeying the Ten Commandments, he is rendering to his country the greatest service. Service of God and service of country are not incompatible. They have the same roots.

Let's not get the idea that patriotism is the exclusive prerogative of the army and navy. It isn't. Patriotism is not a plant that blooms only on the battlefield watered with human blood. Patriotism can flourish in peace as well as in war, and it ought to be in evidence in our everyday activity.

Patriotism is a virtue that comes under that category of virtues known as "piety." It is a practical love of one's country which is not to be stored away until times of danger. Piety is to pervade daily living. Properly understood, it links heaven, home, and country. Patriotism cannot ignore the home because that is the basic unit of the state. Neither state nor home can ignore God because he is the very reason for their existence.

One day Constantius, the father of Constantine the Great, called before him all the Christians of the land and demanded, under pain of death, that each one give up his faith. Some, hoping to retain their positions and save their lives, denied their faith. Others were willing to give up their livelihood and even their lives, rather than deny their faith. Constantius dismissed those who denied their faith and retained in his service those who had been faithful and refused to give up so great a treasure. He believed, he said, that those who were faithful to their God would most likely be faithful to their king.

You must obey the governing authorities. Since all government comes from God, the civil authorities were appointed by God, and so anyone who resists authority is rebelling against God's decision, and such an act is bound to be punished (ROM. 13, 1-2).

59 UPHILL BATTLE

One day the devil decided to sell out. He was going to have a fire sale. He polished all his tools until they glistened brightly in the light of the fires of hell. He put a price tag on each and put them on display. There was pride, gluttony, lust, envy, and all the way down the list. In the corner was a beat-up, wedge-shaped instrument. No matter how he tried, old Nick could not make it shine because it was worn down. Oddly enough it had the highest price tag on it. When questioned about it, he said, "That is my most effective instrument. When everything else fails that will always do the trick. That is discouragement."

How true it is. When everything else fails all Satan has to do is whisper: "What's the use? Why beat your brains out? You're getting nowhere. Why don't you give up?"

We are all tempted at times to give in to discouragement. We easily get our fill of this spiritual combat and wrestling against odds. We are tempted to call it quits. But if we do, we are playing right into the hands of the devil.

Sure, things are tough. That is the price of belonging to the human race. Christ did not promise an easy life. He calls special attention to the fact of the cross. He makes this the mark of his followers: "If anyone will be my disciple, let him deny himself, take up his cross daily and follow me." So, we can expect uphill work. However, we don't have to do it alone. Thinking we have to do it alone often is the reason for discouragement. If we limit our horizon to ourselves, there is no wonder that we give in to discouragement. We know our own weakness and limitations well enough and if this is all we have to rely upon, there may be good reason for wanting to throw in the towel.

There is always God. When St. Paul was on the point of "despairing of life itself," Christ responded "my grace is sufficient for you." Despite the "God is dead" philosophy, God is still very much alive. But he is not going to force himself into our lives. We have to take the initiative and open our hearts and heads to him. Hand in hand with God we can go through life with confidence.

When Satan hangs out his "Fire Sale" sign, we are not buying.

> *Be calm but vigilant, because your enemy the devil is prowling round like a roaring lion, looking for someone to eat. Stand up to him, strong in faith and in the knowledge that your brothers all over the world are suffering the same things* (1 PET. 5, 8-9).

60 CAPACITY LOAD

If idleness is the devil's workshop, then depression of spirit is the devil's high-geared production factory. There is no doubt about it — the devil rejoices whenever he can rob man of his joy of spirit because when a person's spirits are low, there is no telling to what extremes he is liable to go. So many accidents are caused when our spirits are low. So many sins are committed when our spirits are low.

St. Francis of Assisi wrote: "When the spirit is tearful, forlorn, downcast, it is readily swallowed up completely by sadness or it is carried to the extreme of vain enjoyments. If he lingers in his gloom, that Babylonian mess will ripen to the point where, if it is not flushed out with tears, it will generate permanent corrosion in the heart."

Why are we depressed? This question has baffled us for a long time. It is of great concern to the medical profession. The causes are elusive and often demand professional help and long treatment. It does little good to tell a person to "pull himself together" when he can scarcely tolerate even the thought of himself. Serious, deep depression needs competent assistance.

In less serious cases of depression the cause often is the failures in life. If we interpret these failures as a death blow to our self-esteem and self-image, we are crushed. We think poorly of ourselves and become depressed.

We need to be more realistic in understanding ourselves. Failures and mistakes are the common lot of all human beings. If we refuse to accept this fact, we are apt to entertain ambitions beyond our objective potential.

We are not saying that we ought not strive for higher goals. We should. Who is to say what our limits are, if we have the correct motivation? We have no quarrel with high goals. Excessive ambition, however, out of proportion to ability, talents and opportunities can lead to disappointment and depression if we fail to achieve it.

It helps to have true self-knowledge and the ability to laugh at our own foibles and failures. We all have limits. That is the way we are made. If we do the best within those limits, we have a right to be pleased with ourselves because God is pleased.

You have to be patient and not lose heart because the Lord's coming will be soon. If anyone of you is in trouble, he should pray; if anyone is feeling happy he should sing a psalm (JAM. 5, 8-13).

61   SPLINTERS

A man is not a better person just because he has a toothache or a headache. These pains can and often do make him churlish and inconsiderate of those around him. When we are in misery, we want the whole world to know how much we suffer. Of itself pain does not unite us with Christ. The recurring complaint of sick people is their inability to pray. "I just can't concentrate!"

It is a real struggle to look benignly upon the world and even upon Divine Providence when a heavy cross is burrowing into our shoulder. And still, are we to admit that all this suffering which comes into every man's life is futile and vain? It is difficult to believe that this universal experience is just a mistake of creation.

Of all the means that Christ could have chosen to redeem the world, and the choice was limitless, he chose suffering. Is there an intrinsic, necessary connection between suffering and redemption? I don't know. However, the fact that Christ chose suffering as the means of redemption, adds a new dimension to suffering. There is something in it that bears a relationship to almighty God. It is this relationship that I must try to understand, otherwise there is frustration and despair.

The more I think about it the more I am convinced that there is a lot of wasted suffering in the world. There are too many crosses that never become crucifixes, and the difference between a cross and a crucifix is Christ. There are aching feet not united with Christ's pierced feet. Aching hands not united with Christ's punctured hands. Aching heads not united with Christ's thorn-crowned head. Aching hearts not united with Christ's transfixed heart. All these sufferings are flotsam and jetsam unless in some way we make them splinters of the cross of Calvary.

Suffering, as Bishop Sheen says, is like an unsigned check. United with the suffering of Christ, it is endorsed with his signature. Then it takes on incalculable value.

> "Let us not then by impatience
> Mar the beauty of the whole
> But for love of Jesus bear all
> In the silence of our soul.
> Asking Him for grace sufficient
> To sustain us through each loss
> And to treasure each small offering
> As a splinter from His cross."

62   THE GAME OF LIFE

Poor Jim Marshall. He may never live it down. It happened in the Minnesota - San Francisco pro football game. Jim Marshall picked up a fumble and with a sudden burst of speed made a beeline for the goal post. The crowd was shouting thunderously and his teammates were screaming frantically. This gave Jim the added zest. He dashed into the end zone. When it was all over, Jim Marshall discovered that he had run the wrong way. He had scored for the wrong team. This one is for the books!

But is this freak feat something peculiar to Jim Marshall alone? Aren't there a lot of us running in the wrong direction? Scoring for the wrong team? We hear the crowd we associate with shouting about something. We interpret this as approval and put new energy into our blissful stupidity of running the wrong way, scoring for the wrong side.

Let's stop right here. Dead in our tracks and take a look around. Where are we headed? We have to be going somewhere. We have to have some kind of goal because that is the way we are made. Functionally man is somewhat like a bicycle. A bicycle maintains its balance and equilibrium as long as it is moving toward something. We are so built that if we lack personal goals, we lose our balance and sense of direction.

This is why, in this game of life, we have to bring things into focus and determine what our goal is. Where do we really want to go? If we are just running, we are apt to expend a great deal of energy with nothing to show for our pains. What is worse, we are apt to burn up good energy in unwholesome pursuits.

There is wisdom in the adage, "Look before you leap." God has endowed each of us with some brains and he expects us to use them. The future is not entirely a closed fist. We can ask and answer a few pertinent questions which pry open, just a little, this closed fist. If I continue this course, where will it lead me? Is that where I want to go? What do I want from life? How can I attain what I want? Which is the better way? These are the questions we must ask ourselves sooner or later.

If we are satisfied we are heading in the right direction, then by all means give out with a burst of speed. Bring all your energies to bear. If we are not satisfied, we had better take a sharper look around. We may have to reverse our field, lest we score for the wrong team.

> *As for me, my life is already being poured away as a libation, and the time has come for me to be gone. I have fought the good fight to the end; I have run the race to the finish; I have kept the faith; all there is to come now is the crown of righteousness reserved for me* (2 TIM. 4, 6-7).

63 ORDAINED MEN

St. Francis of Assisi kneeling in the mud to kiss the hands of the unworthy priest of Lombardy manifested in a poignant fashion that to him a priest is chosen from among men in things that pertain to God. He was willing to look beyond the human failings. Ordination certainly does not divest a priest of his human nature. He still retains all the human weaknesses inherent in that human nature. On occasion these weaknesses may show up too blatantly. Need this cause wonder?

Is not the wonder that God should choose such fragile instruments to carry on his work? God could have disposed otherwise, but he chose to ennoble the nature he created by making it his official go-between.

At times the choice may work a strain on the laity. This is especially the case when a priest proves to be less a priest than his dignity demands. Today there are priests who are standing up to be counted in areas where formerly their influence was not felt. We don't question for one moment the right and obligation of priests to try to solve the race question, social injustices, poverty, and related problems. His vocation demands that he shape public conscience, not reflect it. This cannot be done solely from the sheltered confines of the pulpit enunciating fine sounding principles. The temper of our times requires that a priest strain to apply these principles in the very haunts of humanity. Somtimes he has to be right there. Just because his presence may create new problems of misunderstanding does not mean he has to abandon his post. At times we may question the means employed. At times we may counsel greater prudence, but prudence does not mean inertia.

The very nature of our times calls for greater understanding and loyalty of the laity. This is not to say that we have to condone what cannot be condoned. But justice requires that we keep everything in perspective and balance. When we must disagree with our priests, this is not to be an occasion for disrespect. When we disagree with anybody, we must still respect him.

More than anything else this is a time for greater prayer that God will find open minds, willing hearts, and ready hands to carry on the work that he has ordained.

> *Every high priest has been taken out of mankind and is appointed to act for men in their relations with God, to offer gifts and sacrifices for sins; and so he can sympathize with those who are ignorant or uncertain because he too lives in the limitations of weakness* (HEB. 5, 1).

64   GOD LOVES ME

It is no astounding revelation to say that we still do not love God as much as we should. Christ said that we are to love God with our whole heart and mind and soul and strength. This is listed as the first and greatest commandment, but it is more than that. It is the perfection of Christian life. It is the secret of lasting happiness. Still, there are so few people who reach that stage of love.

One reason certainly is human selfishness. We are so bound up with our own little worlds that we seldom give God a tumble except perhaps in a perfunctory way when we can't get out of rendering him worship without risking our eternal salvation. How many people would go to Mass on Sunday if the Church would lift the serious obligation?

A more basic reason why so few fall more deeply in love with God may be that we are not truly convinced that God loves us. It is not a question of believing that God loves us. Most of us believe that. But how many of us realize it? How many of us are really convinced? Do we have the abiding, unwavering, deep, continual conviction that God loves us personally, infinitely?

This conviction is essential. Nothing so stimulates love as the firm knowledge that one is truly loved. It ignites a responsive love.

"I have loved you with an everlasting love, therefore I have drawn you to myself, having mercy on you." God goes to almost desperate ends to convince us of his love. His spokesman, St. Paul, even though he had undergone the severest of temptation and the direst of suffering, keeps repeating, "God loves me, God loves me." He is hopeful that the feeling will be contagious.

In the natural realm God gives us countless proofs of his love. He has given us our eyes, ears, tongue, arms, legs. All this wonderful body-soul equipment which we take so much for granted is a continual manifestation of the love he bears for us individually. Add to this the tremendous gifts of soul and spirit, the share in the very life of God himself, the seeds of immortality planted within our being. These are facts we have to realize more graphically. For once we do realize them, the conviction will grow that God loves me, individually, personally, infinitely. Who can fail to respond?

> We ourselves have known and put our faith in God's love toward ourselves. We are to love, then, because he loved us first (1 JN. 4, 16-19).

65   START COUNTING

Among the passions we possess the most turbulent is anger. It can heat the blood and agitate the spirit so that the brain is not able to function properly.

If you have ever seen someone violently angry, you have seen the devastating effect of anger. It is like a stick of dynamite carried around on our person. There is no telling when it will detonate and leave ruin in its wake.

What complicates the situation is that anger begets anger. If you confront a man with your fists clenched, he will clench his fist in return.

But suppose when someone approaches you with clenched fists, you extend the open palm in friendship; he will have to unclench his fist to shake hands with you. If we refuse to fight anger with anger, but contrariwise, with meekness, not only are we doing the Christian thing but we are preserving peace.

A cannon ball carried on the wings of fury crushes rocks, overthrows strong towers, shatters every hard obstacle that gets in its way. But if it strikes against a woolpack, the softness of the material slows its speed and tames its violence. In like manner, our gentleness and meekness can quiet the rage of another person. "A mild answer turns away wrath," says Scripture.

We don't set Socrates up as an example of virtue but there is an incident in his life which has a bearing on our discussion. Xantippe, his wife, was a veritable shrew. She was constantly finding fault. Whenever she started on a rampage, the old philosopher would leave the house and sit on the steps.

One day, as he sat there after a particularly violent tongue lashing, Xantippe doused him with a bucket of water. Without raising his voice, Socrates remarked "All that thunder in there must produce some rain." He refused to fight back. The storm soon spent itself.

If we are irascible by nature, we cannot take refuge in the thought, "I can't help it; that is the way I am made." We can help it and we ought to get busy.

St. Gregory gives us two little rules to help us. First, when we are crossed and the urge is on us to get even, think of the insults that Christ had to suffer. Compare ours to his. See what he does and draw inspiration from his example.

Second, if it is the shortcomings and failings of others that get on our nerves, consider our own failings and shortcomings and how we get on other people's nerves. We will be more willing to overlook their aggravation.

> *Remember this, my dear brothers: be quick to listen but slow to speak and slow to rouse your temper; God's righteousness is never served by man's anger* (JAM. 1, 19).

Blessed Are the Clean of Heart

66   LIFE AND LOVE

Almighty God could have created each one of us as a full grown man or woman. But he didn't. He chose to share his creative powers with creatures and so he endowed man and woman with the wonderful power of procreation.

This fact points up the dignity of sex. It is not a toy but a sublime sharing in the creative power of God himself.

This power is not something we have in common with animals. Rather animals have it in common with man, and man has it in common with God. This is one of the sublime features of man's makeup.

Because God wanted to guarantee the use of this faculty, he attached a pleasure to its function. Just as God wants man to preserve his life, so he has attached a pleasure to eating.

However, sometimes God asks for the use of this faculty and sometimes he asks the sacrifice of it. This is where the struggle comes in.

Since the fall of man we have lost that complete control over our urges and drives. As a result we seek at times to satisfy this sexual pleasure at a time and in a way not intended by God. This gives rise to conflict within us.

This struggle to keep pleasure within the right limits is compounded by curiosity. The mystery of sex can be enticing and intriguing. Add to this the lax moral code regarding sex which seems all too prevalent, you get some understanding of the dimensions of the problem.

A basic element in any solution to the problem is getting back to a realization of the sublimity of sex. We shield it not because it is bad or taboo, but because it is sacred. We control it not because there is anything wrong with it, but because it is a gift of God.

Since God is the giver, he has a right to tell us when we may use it and when we may not use it. What devotees of sexual laxity forget is that God is still Master of creation. Sex certainly has its place in God's plan. It is up to us to learn first of all what is God's plan and then give sex its proper role.

> *What God wants is for you to be holy. He wants you to keep away from fornication, and each of you to know how to use the body that belongs to him in a way that is holy and honorable, not giving way to selfish lust like the pagans who do not know God* (1 THES. 4, 3-4).

67   CROWN OF VICTORY

You may have heard it put this way before: "In the beginning God created the world; then he rested. Then he created man and rested. Then he created woman and neither God nor man has rested since." This witticism is not completely true but it does point to the historic fact of the fall of man which was the result initially of the curiosity of Eve. Since the fall, a certain

disorder has set in and we all feel a struggle to survive the countless obstacles that beset our path to salvation.

St. Paul put it this way: "I am delighted with the law of God
according to the inward man, but I see another law in my members, fighting against the law of my mind and captivating me
in the law of sin that is in my members" (Rom. 7, 22).

From the moment we learn to distinguish right from wrong,
the struggle begins. Even as children we found it difficult to be
good and easy to be bad. These were our early experiences with
temptation. As we grow older, we meet up with new and more
violent temptations. And there is no letup. There are no exceptions — no age, no place, no time, no state in life is free from
temptations.

We may well wish to be free from temptations, but wishing
will not make it so. Since we cannot escape temptations, we might
just as well make virtue of necessity and draw blessing from
evil.

The first advantage we can get from temptation is the reward
we achieve if we resist successfully. We are not dumped into
heaven. We have to earn that goal and that can be done by overcoming temptations.

Read what St. James writes: "Count it all joy when you shall
fall into divers temptations knowing that the trying of your faith
works patience. Blessed is the man who endures temptations for
when he has been proved, he shall receive the crown of life."

St. Paul writes: "Know you not that they who run in a race,
all indeed run, but one receives the crown. So run that you may
obtain, and everyone that strives for the mastery refrains himself
from all things and they indeed that they may receive a corruptible
crown, but we an incorruptible one." So it is that every mortal
temptation overcome becomes a sparkling gem in our immortal
crown.

*We prove we are servants of God by great fortitude
in times of suffering . . . We prove we are servants
of God by our purity, knowledge, patience and kind-*

ness, by a spirit of holiness, by a love free from affectation (2 COR. 6, 4-6).

68 JUST ONE MOMENT

If we embrace each present moment with all our vital energy so that we reserve little for the past or even the future, there will be little room for fear. The present moment is what matters. God is a jealous God and he demands our whole being at every moment. Often we are too busy about too many things. We are troubled about minutia and yet with all our cares we accomplish so little.

How often we are troubled about possible future events. Because of our anxiety, we miss the actual present moment. In the end, matters turn out so differently from what we had expected. Our worries are in vain.

How often we are troubled about probable future suffering. Some people have even broken down under this strain because they did not possess the grace to bear the burden of the future suffering. Let's always keep this in mind: we possess the necessary grace for the present moment.

In his goodness, God has concealed the future from our eyes. We are too weak to bear its burdens. Only a few very strong souls were able to see the future, but they too nearly broke under that strain.

The best care for the future is not to care. If we make the best use of the present moment, we can "cast our cares upon the Lord." By fulfilling the whole duty of the present moment, we receive the grace we need for the next. If it brings pain and sorrow, it also brings grace. "God is faithful and will not permit you to be tempted beyond your strength, but with the temptation, will also give you a way out that you may be able to bear it."

If only we would stop interfering with God's providence. We only spoil things. The whole creation is an immense work of art which continually issues from the hand of God. His wisdom shines forth in its harmony. Our life is but a tiny fragment of the whole. We are ignorant of God's plan concerning ourselves and more so, of our position and significance in the total scheme of things. Since we do not know how we are interwoven into the intricate pattern of the threads that knit together the past and the future, the best course of action is to entrust ourselves entirely to the guidance of God. He gives us but one moment at a time, the moment to be used to the best of our ability.

> *We beg you once again not to neglect the grace of God you have received. Well, now is the favorable time; this is the day of salvation* (2 COR. 6, 1-2).

69   HE PROVIDES

As our Father, God has supreme authority over us; ours is the obligation to obey. More than that though, God is also our supreme provider. One of the chief characteristics of a good father is to provide for the welfare of his children. In the natural order God has provided for us very well. He has given us the wonderful faculties of sight, touch, taste, hearing, and smell. Through our senses, life can be a pleasant experience. He has also given us the corresponding creatures that delight the senses. The grandeur of a sunset, the whisper of a breeze in the forest, the perfume of spring, the warmth of a kiss, the delicious crunch of an apple — these are some of the natural provisions. Our lungs will always find the correct mixture in the atmosphere to keep life going. The seasons will change and the crops will grow to provide food for our table. God has provided for our natural life abundantly.

In the supernatural order God is no less provident. The graces merited by Christ on Calvary are distributed so conveniently through the seven sacraments. At every turning point in our life there is a sacrament to nurture and sustain our supernatural life. The greatest provision is the "supersubstantial" Bread that we may receive often, even daily, if we choose.

Because the saints realized in a vivid way that God was the Provider, they took him at his word. They cast their cares upon the Lord. St. Francis was willing to depend solely on Divine Providence. Without reluctance he could abandon all those things that the world depends upon and which in many cases are found wanting.

Because they were willing to take God at his word and let him provide, the saints were the greatest optimists in the world. No matter how man tries to interfere, God is still running this world. Because the saints were so thoroughly convinced of that fact, they were never downcast. Theirs was an optimism not of feeling because that is beyond control, but an optimism of conviction.

There is nothing more pleasing to God then to be recognized as our great Provider. That is why, even though he knows our needs, he still wants us to ask. It takes but a brief reflection to recall how well God has provided for us. Time without number, we have experienced his loving care in the natural order but above all in the supernatural order. This knowledge ought to make us confirmed optimists by conviction.

Make no mistake about this, my dear brothers, it is all that is good, everything that is perfect, which is given from above; it comes down from the Father of all light (JAM. 1, 16-17).

70   FLAMING YOUTH

Do you think the saints were a bunch of old fogies? What is the average age of the saints? "Who cares?" Is that what you are saying? Well, just for kicks try to find out.

It might come as a surprise to learn there are some people in the world who take God seriously long before they make a down-payment on their burial lot. Sure, we know what the wise guys of the mod age are saying: "Life is my oyster. I will suck out the meat, then God can have the empty shell." What kind of sop is that to hand someone on whom we depend for everything we are and everything we have? If we put off turning to God until we are too old to get any kick out of sin, what makes anyone think almighty God is going to accept a bargain like that? I wouldn't place any odds on it.

When you cut through all this pose and pretense, who has more to gain than the young when they throw in their lot with God. Youth is an important period of life. It is a time of mood and mystery, when a budding personality experiences strange emotions and solitary conflicts as he seeks his niche in the adult world. It is a time of troubled, wistful looks into the future, trying to catch a glimpse of what that closed fist holds.

Throughout this state of ferment young people flame with energy and enthusiasm. But there is the danger of young people burning themselves out in ignoble pursuits. There is eagerness, ambition, optimism. This is a stage that has so many plus signs capable of splendid achievement only if pointed in the right direction.

All that it really takes is just a little shift of the center of our focus. Young people must think of the future. Granted. There is nothing particularly wrong in working for money and fame. Granted. Young people do not have to spend all their time on other people's problems. Grant that too. But may we ask, how much effort will it really take to make God the center around which our lives pivot? How much extra effort will it take to do some of the wonderful unselfish things we associate with the saints? A completely unselfish life of serving God in others is not beyond the powers of young people. This kind of life is more worthy of the God we love, more like the Christ who as a young man had done so much for us. When you are measured for your coffin, it is too late.

> Remember your creator in the days of your youth, before evil days come and the years approach when you say, 'These give me no pleasure' (ECCLE. 12, 1).

71   GIVE ME ROOM

As he entered the room the cry went up, "Make room for Col. Davey Crockett." Above the din his voice boomed out, "Nobody makes room for Davey Crockett. Davey Crockett makes room for himself." This was the stuff of which the early pioneers were made. We stand in awe of their independence; we are proud that they stamped America with their character.

There was a time when a person who wanted something went to work and earned it. If your father or grandfather lost his job, he did not sit around on his apathy and wait for a government handout. He struck out on his own. He took whatever job was at hand. He would travel miles, spend hours, if there was honest work available.

Today we stage a riot to get what we want — at somebody else's expense. Many people in real need will not accept a job unless it is to their liking or convenient to their dwelling.

The hardy immigrants who built this nation were seeking one thing only — the opportunity to make their own way. The very idea of "something for nothing" was an abomination. To accept the earnings of others without exerting their own strength rubbed against the grain. Today, judging from the conduct of many people one would believe the only worthwhile principle is — get as much as you can with the least amount of exertion.

It used to take a lifetime of honest hard work and thrift for a family to accumulate a modicum of security. The hard work did not hurt them and they felt a sense of great pride. They were productive. Sad to say, this spirit is on the wane. All over this land of ours are people who think that the world owes them a living. What is worse they do not hesitate to use foul means to vindicate their claim.

One of the by-products of an affluent society is a perversion of values. We are able to mass produce just about everything except character, that healthy independence of judgment and action that is so frightfully needed today. In some way, once again we have to develop self-respect that accepts the scriptural injunction "by the sweat of your brow" not as a curse but as a challenge.

> *Our one desire is that every one of you should go on showing the same earnestness to the end, to the perfect fulfilment of our hopes, never growing careless, but imitating those who have the faith and the perseverance to inherit the promises* (HEB. 6, 11-12).

72   CONTAGIOUS

On my way to Mass one morning I noticed a stranger approaching me. He was grim and determined. It was obvious that he was intent on passing by without a greeting. I let him go by without a nod. The next morning I saw him again. Again it was evident he was going to give me the cold shoulder. When he got abreast of me, I quietly said: "Good morning." This startled him and he mumbled a greeting in response, almost ashamed of having been caught off-guard. The third morning as he approached me, he was smiling broadly and greeted me cheerfully.

I tried to evaluate the experience. Most probably what this man was doing was reflecting myself to me. Perhaps I had given him the impression that I was preoccupied and had no intention of greeting him. He reflected this attitude by passing by without a greeting. When I approached him with a friendlier air, he reflected this friendliness too.

I am convinced that we can elicit from the people we deal with just about any emotion or reaction we desire by first registering it ourselves. By way of experiment, study the people coming toward you. Don't they mirror back to you the same expression you have on your face? If you are grim, determined, preoccupied, you will see the same written on their features. Try smiling. Notice how that smile bounces right back to you. Then turn around and see how that smile has been passed on to the very next person.

Kruschev once issued an order that the Russians were to try to smile more. He realized, I suppose, that friendliness had its advantages. Friendliness does pay off. Every salesman knows that. For Christians, however, the overtures of friendliness and good cheer should spring from a more important reason. We are dealing with children of God. The human personality has a worth all its own. That is a blood brother approaching, nurtured by the blood of Christ. We all belong to the same family of God and certainly members of our family have the first claim on our friendliness. After all we have heard the glad tidings and should want to share them with everyone we meet. The Christian kinship that we recognize ought to shine forth in our eyes and on our lips. We should be radiating the friendliness of Christ. This too is a big part of the Christian apostolate.

> *Rejoice with those who rejoice and be sad with those in sorrow. Treat everyone with equal kindness; never be condescending but make real friends with the poor* (ROM. 12, 15-16).

73 DEAR-DROPS

It is odd how some people try to excuse their own glumness. How can we be happy and cheerful when we live in a "vale of tears"? We use these very words when we pray the *Salve Regina*.

To be sure we are living in a vale of tears to the extent that there are barriers obstructing our path to heaven, to the extent that there are enemies to overcome. It might be well, however, to remember the words of Savonarola: "If there were no enemies, there would be no fight. If there were no fight, there would be no victory. If there were no victory, there would be no crown." We know how St. Paul rejoiced in a battle well fought.

On the other hand, however, I'm not so sure we are living in an unqualified vale of tears. There are countless little joys in nature. If we get the dust out of our eyes, we can see a vast panorama . . . the chirping birds, the purling brooks, the luxuriant verdure, the twinkling stars, the smiling sun, the fleecy snow-drops that remind us of star dust. There is a super-abundance of little joys in nature.

Let's look at the line of reasoning of the famous theologian, John Duns Scotus. When almighty God decided to create, at the dawn of eternity, he had in mind to create first and foremost, Christ. Christ was to serve as the prototype, the blueprint for the rest of creation.

Just as the prism splinters the golden sunlight into the riotous colors of the rainbow, so the prism of God's creative love splintered the perfections of Christ and fashioned the various kingdoms according to them. Thus, Christ's perfections became the motif of creation. In Christ's resplendent soul, for example, God saw mirrored the choirs of the angles. After Christ's perfect body all visible creation was sculptured. The stars that collect in the milky galaxies, the cataracts that dash in silvery spray over the precipices, the flowers wooed by the babbling brook, the sun that shines with soothing brilliance, all have captured a gleam of Christ's perfection, have imprisoned a spark of his charm. God spoke and all creation became a sparkling monstrance to enshrine the heart of Christ our King.

This idea the saints realized. That is why they found such joy in creation. Everything about them spoke about God. Everywhere they saw footprints of their Divine Master. Do you see why I'm not so sure we live in a "vale of tears."

He is the radiant light of God's glory and the perfect copy of his nature, sustaining the universe by his powerful command: *So he is now as far above the angels as the title which he has inherited is higher than their own name* (HEB. 1, 3-4).

74   WHO ARE YOU?

One advantage we can gain from temptations is valuable self-knowledge. Self-knowledge is one of the greatest aids to growth in virtue and perfection. It is only by knowing ourselves that we can concentrate our efforts towards making progress. Without this self-knowledge we do a lot of shadow-boxing which is a waste of energy.

From the nature of our temptations, from their frequency and intensity, we can learn our weak points, our dominating vices, our chief character defects. We can also learn how fragile and weak we are and how, without the help of God, we are easily broken.

Suppose a person is constantly plagued with vanity and pride. These vices pummel him at every turn. These temptations will emphasize his dire need for the virtue of humility. Suppose a person is irked by the slightest injury, real or imaginary. Suppose he is prone to impatience and irritation with or without provocation. From this experience he learns his need for patience and meekness. Suppose a person is haunted by temptations against purity which ceaselessly color his thoughts and intrude even into the innocent things of life. From this he learns his need for discipline and mortification.

Regardless what our temptations may be, whether we are forever viewing life through the green glasses of envy, or too indolent to react to worthy inspiration, or given to carping criticism, miserliness, rashness, or indifference, they all give us a clearer understanding of ourselves. With this knowledge as a starting point, we can chart a course of action that will bring us closer to God.

We can look upon temptations either as a trial and test, or as a seduction and an inducement to sin. In the sense of a trial or test, we can say that God does at times put us to a test. We know this from the incident in the life of Abraham when God ordered him to sacrifice his only son. This was a test of faith. In the life of Job, we see that God allowed serious afflictions to befall him in order to teach the important lesson of patience.

As a seduction or inducement to sin, however, it would be blasphemy to attribute temptation to God. St. James tells us: "Let no man, when he is tempted, say that he is tempted by God. For God is not a tempter to evil and he tempts no man." As inducements to sin, temptations come from ourselves, our neighbors, and the devil. No matter what the source of temptation, we are bound to resist energetically and in our resistance learn the important lesson of self-knowledge.

> *Happy the man who stands firm when trials come. He has proved himself and will win the prize of life, the crown that the Lord has promised to those who love him* (JAM. 1, 12).

75 GRACE'S FOUNDATION

You can't build on quicksand. It is evident that we need some kind of solid foundation. Without it the first strong gust of wind will sweep away whatever it is you are building. We all know this. But do we also know that in this business of building a worthwhile life we need a solid foundation on which to build?

There has to be a solid *natural* foundation on which to build the supernatural. Grace perfects nature, which means that in the ordinary course of events what we have by nature forms the basis of our supernature. Grace found in Francis, for example, certain natural endowments which were eventually refined and reformed and in the process he became a great saint.

What we are saying is that a person must first of all have character. In each of us there is a distinctive mark that stamps our personality. This is our character. One may have lofty ambitions, noble aspirations, a dignified bearing and inviolable sincerity. His would be fine character. Another may reveal vile inclinations, coarse tendencies, selfishness and lack of consideration. His would be a low character. We run the gamut from the best to the worst.

These external manifestations that we can observe emanate from the inner man. Behind it all coloring his daily activity is the source of his power — his will. To possess will power is to possess character.

Lacordaire writes: "Character is a secret and persistent energy of will, a sort of fixed steadiness of purpose, a still greater steadiness of being true to one's friendships, to one's virtues."

Guibert says: "If life is a flood of active energies, it is character that hollows the river bed for the flowing stream. If life is a task to fulfill, character is the power which accumulates its resources and applies them to the work ordained."

Each of us has received our quota of will power from our Creator. It is a natural endowment. But it is a seedling. It has to be developed. Not to develop it is to waste it. The way in which we develop it or the way in which others help us develop it will determine in large measure the kind of supernatural life we perfect.

If we accept the premise that the supernatural builds on the natural, it follows that whatever we do to improve nature will prove advantageous to our supernatural life.

   . . . *we pray continually that God will make you worthy of his call, and by his power fulfil all your*

*desires for goodness and complete all that you have
been doing through faith . . . (2 THES. 1, 11).*

76   GOD IS LOVE

St. John tells us, "God is love." This means that God is not
only capable of loving, but is love itself. God and love are identical. This goes back to the infinite nature of God. Over simplified
this means what God *has* he *is*. So God not only has love; he is
love. Since God is infinite and supreme, God as love is likewise
infinite and supreme.

It is the nature of love to communicate its goodness to others.
A man who truly loves his neighbor will communicate his goodness by kind words, charitable thoughts and good deeds. This is
how love operates. It can't sit still. It must overflow.

So God as love must overflow. He has communicated his goodness to us first of all by creation. Our very existence and the existence of the things around us are manifestations of God's goodness and love. God's love has overflowed into creation in a
thousand different ways, but the greatest proof of this love is
found in the Incarnation. "God so loved the world as to send his
only begotten Son."

In a way we all sense that the coming of Christ is the greatest
sign of God's goodness and love. We celebrate his coming with
a great deal of ceremony. We look upon Christmas as one of the
most joyous feasts. This is certainly as it should be. However,
Christmas decorations are soon removed, carols soon die out, and
cribs put away. All safely stored to be hauled out again next
December. We wonder if with these trappings we also pack away

Anyone who understands what his faith has to offer will know
that every day is Christmas. The effects of Christ's coming remains
with us throughout the year. There is so much in our daily lives
that is directly related to his coming. But don't we tend to live our

lives as if Christ had not come? Our trouble may be a lack of appreciation of this tremendous idea of St. John, "God is love." Love in all its shapes and misshapes is a moving force in every life. If we can only convince ourselves that God is love in its truest and deepest sense and that Christ's coming is the most eloquent expression of that love, we would have a formula for Christ-consciousness which will endure throughout the entire year.

> *This was to show for all ages to come, through his goodness toward us in Christ Jesus, how infinitely rich he is in grace. Because it is by grace that you have been saved, through faith, not by anything of your own, but by a gift from God* (EPH. 2, 7-8).

77   HUB OF LIFE

St. Francis of Assisi wrote: "I beg you all to show every reverence and honor possible to the most holy Body and Blood of our Lord Jesus Christ in whom all things in heaven and on earth are set at peace and are reconciled."

It is no strain on our logic to see Christ in the Eucharist as the center of the universe, especially if we accept the thinking of John Duns Scotus. Briefly it is this: Christ's coming was no afterthought. Once God decided to create, he had in mind to create Christ first and foremost. St. Paul calls him the "firstborn of the creatures." Not the firstborn in time but the firstborn in intention. As the "firstborn" he was to serve as the prototype of the rest of creation in the sense that everything else in creation was molded according to some perfection of Christ. Everywhere we look we can find a gleam of the perfection of Christ.

More than this, Christ was to serve as the goal, the purpose of all creation. ". . . for all things are yours . . . and you are Christ's and Christ is God's."

When we study the life of Christ, we see that he took great pains to prepare his followers for his Eucharistic presence. After the multiplication of loaves, when the crowd found him in Capharnaum, he informed them in no uncertain terms: "I am the bread which came down from heaven." "And the bread which I will give for the life of the world is my flesh." Despite the appalled consternation that ensued, he did not retract a single word.

When we come to the Last Supper, we get the idea that this was what Christ was waiting for. "I have desired earnestly to eat this passover with you" — as if now his life had reached its climax. It was at this precise moment that he instituted the Blessed Sacrament. One cannot help getting the impression that this was the culmination of his life. Everything pointed toward it.

If then Christ is all that we said in the words of Duns Scotus and the institution of the Eucharist was the zenith of his life, it follows that Christ in the Eucharist is the prototype and purpose of all creation. Right there in the tabernacle is the hub around which everything in life must revolve if it is going to have true meaning.

I am the living bread which has come down from heaven. Anyone who eats this bread will live forever; and the bread that I shall give is my flesh, for the life of the world (JN. 6, 51).

78   SMALL BEGINNINGS

When I was a little boy, somebody gave me a bottle with a large cucumber in it. The neck of the bottle was so small and the cucumber so large that I could not figure out how in the world the cucumber got in there.

My puzzlement was solved when, out in the garden, I came across a bottle slipped over a tiny green cucumber still on the vine. Then I understood.

We often see men and women walking around with bad habits and wonder how any strong sensible person could be a victim of such stupid conduct.

The cucumber in the bottle gives us a clue. These habits grew on them from the time they were young. No attempt was made to rid themselves of these habits. Or what attempts were made to help them, were shrugged off.

Now we have the problem. I say "we" because every habit that besets a person in some way will affect the circles in which he moves. To the extent that it affects that circle, it becomes more than his problem. It becomes our problem. Perhaps we will not be able to do anything about the situation if the bad habit belongs to somebody else. At best, we can learn to live with it; and where the opportunity presents itself, give a tactful nudge now and then with the hope that the person with the bad habit will do something about it.

On the other hand, if examination reveals in us a habit that may have grown imperceptibly until it has reached huge proportions and we are a downright nuisance to the people around us, it is up to us to do something about it. The habit is there and it has grown like the cucumber. The only way we can extricate it, is by cutting it to pieces. This is the brutal process we must undertake. In a certain sense we have to be our own executioner. Many times we are reluctant to undertake the job because of the violence involved so we go through life hampered in our efforts to be good and do good. Sacred Scripture however, does not tolerate this namby-pamby attitude. The kingdom of heaven is subjected to violence and the violent are taking it by storm. If your right eye is a source of scandal pluck it out. If your arm gets in the way of doing good, cut it off. If anything, scripture is telling us to get with it even if there is sacrififce involved.

You cannot belong to Christ Jesus unless you crucify all self-indulgent passions and desires (GAL. 5, 24).

79   AS YOU TRAVEL ASK US

Striving to improve our spiritual life is often compared to climbing a mountain we must ever be on our guard to avoid a misstep that may result in a fatal fall. To avoid such a fall in the spiritual life we suggest several powerful means.

First, there is spiritual direction. If you want to travel quickly from city to city you have to get on the main road and stick to it. If you do not know where that road is, you ask someone who knows. On every confessional door and rectory should hang the sign, "As You Travel Ask Us."

"Those who seek to climb the mountain of perfection, are more exposed to mistakes, precisely because they ascend less frequented paths and because of this they need a master and guide more than others" (Pope Leo XIII).

Second, great confidence in God's love and in the power of grace and Divine Providence. We must never forget that heaven is much more interested in our progress than even we ourselves. Since it is God's will that we scale the heights, it is a foregone conclusion that he will be on hand to give us the help we need. We need a little more of the confidence of St. Paul who wrote: "I can do all things in him who strengthens me."

Third, familiarity with the saints. Example means much in life. We are greatly influenced by the example of those around us. Many times we don't perceive the influence. If we surround ourselves with examples of great sacrifice and eminent holiness, we certainly will benefit from the relationship. Seeing how other human beings were able to make the grade, we take courage to keep on trying in spite of obstacles. For this reason it is important that we get acquainted with our big brothers and sisters.

Fourth, devotion to the Holy Spirit. It is the function of the Holy Spirit not only to guide the Church but to direct the faithful on the path of perfection. Cardinal Mercier tells us that "whoever is guided by the Holy Spirit will attain marvelous heights of sanctity." We are not in this battle alone. We have so much working in our favor if only we understand who our allies are.

My brothers, be united in following my rule of life. Take as your models everybody who is already doing this and study them as you used to study us (PHIL. 3, 17).

80   *FOUNT OF WISDOM*

When Satan tempted Christ in the desert, Christ fended off each temptation with a quotation from Sacred Scripture. Often during his public life he referred to the Old Testament in order to make a point. When he languished on the cross, snatches of Scripture were heard from his parched lips. So often did Christ call upon Scripture that one gets the impression that from his youth Scripture must have formed a part of his daily life. Not only did he hear it in the home at Nazareth, but he meditated on it deeply.

Are we to follow in the footsteps of Christ? There is no more important way than drinking from the founts of wisdom, the Sacred Scriptures. In St. Paul's letter to Timothy we read: "The Holy Scriptures can instruct you to salvation by the faith which is in Christ Jesus. All Scripture, inspired of God, is profitable to teach, to reprove, to correct, to instruct in justice that the man of God may be perfect, furnished for every good work."

To read the word of God is to encounter Christ. As often as we expose ourselves to the word of God, it works on our heart and soul. There is a certain charismatic character to Scripture which, if read with the proper disposition, can transform the human heart. Daily, if possible, we ought to try to encounter Christ in the Word of God. This is how we can become thoroughly familiar with the word of God and the spirit of Christ. Profound scholarship is not a prerequisite because there is so much of Scripture that is easily understood and of sufficient inspiration that one need not break his head over the more difficult passages. These we can just as well leave to the scholars. Let us learn to read the word of God with simplicity, faith, and love. Perhaps then we too will come away from this encounter with Christ feeling like the disciples on their way to Emmaus, "Was not our heart burning within us as he was speaking?"

> *All scripture is inspired by God and can profitably be used for teaching, for refuting error, for guiding people's lives and teaching them to be holy. This is how the man who is dedicated to God becomes fully equipped and ready for any good work* (2 TIM. 3, 16-17).

81   HIDDEN HELPS

"Who will roll away the stone?" This is the question that plagued the women on their way to the tomb early Sunday morning. They expected to find an obstacle preventing their service of charity to the dead. Relying on their own strength, they knew that they could not cope with the obstacle. So they were greatly concerned. The last thing they expected was a special intervention of God. Had they read Scripture correctly, had they listened more attentively to the words of the Master, perhaps they would not now be in this quandary.

Soon enough they discovered that their great concern was in vain because when they arrived at the tomb, they found that the great stone was already rolled away.

So many of us go through life expecting obstacles. Many times we magnify their size. Relying on our own strength, we are often discouraged even before we tackle the problem. "Who will roll away the stone?", we ask ourselves with a feeling of futility. We are so sure the stone is there and so sure that it cannot be removed.

What we often fail to understand is that God still has a hand in running this world. If we are not attentive to his message or discount his power, then life can be filled with all sorts of un-movable stones which will discourage us. "Who will roll away the stone?" This question is asked over and over again. Why don't we learn the lesson that is so obvious in the Easter morning episode? With a little more faith and a little more hope we will find that the stone has already been rolled away.

This is one of the side-lessons of the Easter event which is so often overlooked. But still it is one from which we can gain a great deal of encouragement and confidence. St. Paul reaffirms the lesson when he says: "God is faithful and will not permit you to be tempted beyond your strength, but with the temptation will give you a way out that you may be able to bear it."

> *In the world you will have trouble, but be brave: I have conquered the world* (JN. 16, 32).

82 GET WITH IT*

"I know it, but I can't explain it!" This is the timeworn alibi of the schoolboy. Equally familiar is the reply of the teacher: "If you can't put it into words, you simply do not know it." This is a generally valid rule of thumb. If you cannot communicate your idea, you do not have a firm grasp on it.

St. Francis of Assisi used to say, "So much a man knows as he puts into practice." He is saying the same thing as the teacher. You don't really know a truth until you have attempted to put it to work in your life.

The saints would say, "No humility without humiliation." This is true of all the other virtues — charity, patience, fortitude, purity. We simply must get beyond the discussion stage. We have to get in there and dirty our hands in the spiritual and corporal works of mercy before we really know them.

We add a dimension to our knowledge of a truth when we actually get involved in living it. Our education is not complete until we get down from the ivory tower of theory into the market place of practice. Patience and meekness are not practiced at the writing desk or in the study. They are encountered and known on the crowded bus, in the workshop, in the study hall, at family gatherings.

Too many of us are like Ivan in *Brothers Karamazov* who said: "I could never understand how one can love one's neighbor. It's just one's neighbor, to my mind, that one can't love, though one might love those at a distance. For anyone to love a man, he must be hidden, for as soon as he shows his face, love is gone. A man is rarely ready to admit another's suffering. Why don't he admit it, do you think? Because I smell unpleasant, because I have a stupid face, because I have trod on his foot. One can love one's neighbor in the abstract, but at close quarters it is almost impossible."

Easy or hard, we have to become involved; a man who does not merely talk ideals but puts them to test in the laboratory of everyday living. This was Christ. What he preached he had already practiced. He had experienced the difficulties involved in achievement. He knew the struggle. He fully appreciated those who succeeded and had the utmost sympathy for those who failed.

---

*From *Third Order Bulletin,* Franciscan Herald Press, Chicago.

> *To attain this you will have to do your utmost your-
> selves, adding goodness to the faith you have, under-
> standing to your goodness, self-control to your under-
> standing, patience to your self-control, true devotion
> to your patience, kindness toward your fellowmen to
> your devotion, and, to this kindness, love* (2 PET. 5, 7).

83 WEAK OR MEEK

"That's ridiculous!" This is what ran through the mind of the crowd as they listened to the speaker say, "Blessed are the meek for they shall possess the land." They were used to hearing and living by the sensible standard of "an eye for an eye and a tooth for a tooth." Now Christ comes along with a perfectly preposterous point. "I say to you not to resist evildoers. On the contrary, if someone strikes you on the right cheek, turn to him the other also. And if anyone would go to law with you and take your tunic, let him take your cloak as well." This was too much for them to stomach.

Is this same attitude not reflected in the minds of a lot of modern people? Nobody in his right mind will make a case for turning the other cheek. Who wants to be meek? Don't we look upon a meek person as colorless, without energy and spirit? Someone who gets pushed around and stepped on with contempt? Don't we associate a taint of cowardice with meekness?

But when you think about it, would the virile Christ recommend and bless anything that smacked of cowardice and weakness?

When you think about it further, the meekness that the world spurns is a caricature of the real virtue. True meekness is not mousyness or spineless passivity. It is not making a doormat of oneself. It is not the same as a sluggish, indolent temperament that is hard to arouse even when principles are at stake.

Meekness is a strong virtue. It demands steady discipline and self-control. It is self-possession. A weak person can never be meek because a weak person can never control the surging power of anger. A weak person could never direct all that energy into worthy channels.

A meek person will fight. He will get angry. But at the right time and in the right place and in the right way. There is a big difference. Selfishness and self-love are behind the person who is not meek. His temper will rise as soon as his ego is piqued or his pride humbled. Not so the truly meek person. He will not raise his voice or clench his fist or vent his spleen each time his sensitivity or vanity is dealt a stinging blow. He keeps a firm grip on his energy until something more sacred is at issue. He is guided by a keen sense of right and wrong. He will fight when principles are at stake and just enough to vindicate those principles.

Who is stronger? The one who loses his head at the slightest provocation or the one who keeps his head in the midst of even serious provocation? Who has command of the situation? Who possesses the land? This is the difference between the weak and the meek.

> *Love your enemies, do good to those who hate you, bless those who curse you, pray for those who treat you badly. To the man who slaps you on one cheek, present the other cheek too* (LK. 6, 27-28).

84   STAY WITH IT

Harry Golden writes: If studies had been taken in the Roman Empire in 65 A.D. on religious preferences, they would have shown 51 per cent for Jupiter, 30 for Zeus, about 9 for Mithra and about one per cent for Jesus. So St. Paul, who was promoting Jesus, might have just gone home and said the heck with it. But Paul stayed — and that made the difference."

Paul stayed on the job and that made the difference. He did not sit around bemoaning the odds — and they were great against him. He did not quit because his percentage was slim. He did not ask for preferential treatment. He had a job to do and stayed with it through all kinds of hardships. "We were crushed beyond measure — beyond our strength so that we were weary even of life." The tribulations, distresses, strifes, sleepless nights, fasting, beatings, imprisonment were no slight temptation for him to throw in the towel. But Paul stayed on the job and that made the difference.

We all have it tough. Everything in life that is worthwhile has its price of "sweat and tears and blood." The big difference between the person who succeeds and the person who fails is not fewer obstacles or an easier course. The successful ones stayed on the job and that is what made the difference. They stayed on the job despite the agony and frustrations. They refused to say "no" in the face of great opposition. Even though their chances of success were slim they disdained the thought of defeat. They stayed on the job.

You know the story of the two frogs that fell into a pail of cream. They paddled around for a while in a futile attempt to get out. Finally, one of them said, "I've had it" and sank to the bottom. The other stayed on the job. He thrashed about and paddled furiously until, to his surprise the cream turned to butter and he was able to jump out. A fable? Yes. But take another look. What made the difference?

How often have we not heard someone say, after he had given up, "If only I had held on just a little longer."

Is it a job? Is it a marriage? Is it a bad habit? Is it a struggle to be good? Are these the things that are bugging you? We all are tempted to give up. But let's picture ourselves five years from now, or ten years. How different will the picture be if we stay on the job now? Did Christ not say something about those who persevere to the bitter end?

> *Keep running steadily in the race you have started. Let us not lose sight of Jesus . . . Think of the way he stood such opposition from sinners and then you will not give up for want of courage* (HEB. 12, 2-3).

85   A STORMY AFFAIR

When the apostles entered the boat at the bidding of Christ, there was no thought of storms or danger. The peaceful quiet of nature lay over the world and the Master himself fell asleep. Without warning the whole scene is changed. A violent gust of wind comes gushing down from the heights, followed by others more violent. The storm is upon them with all its fury, lashing the waters into a fierce uproar. The boat is tossed to and fro like a helpless ball.

Fighting back the panic and terror, the apostles bend every muscle and nerve to combat the elements. In spite of their best efforts, the storm is too much for them. A cry of distress resounds, "Lord, save us."

This hour of distress was the school in which the apostles were to learn a lesson for life. They were to be made conscious of their strength; at the same time they were to become conscious of their weakness. In the end, the help of the Lord was at hand.

In like manner, suffering and affliction gives up a schooling. The storms and tribulations that arise in our lives are intended for our instruction. At these times our Lord seems to be asleep; we do not sense his presence. He seems to have abandoned us to let us fight the storm alone. In a way this is necessary for we have to become conscious of our power. But in the very same experience we are made to realize our weakness and humbly acknowledge it. When our strength fails, then we believe in help from God.

The storms and tribulations are an important and useful school in which we often learn more in a few hours than we do otherwise in weeks and months of tranquility. In storms and stresses many self-delusions vanish from our minds and we learn to know ourselves. So when they come, and come they will, do not push the panic button.

> *Happy the man who stands firm when trials come.*
> *He has proved himself and will win the prize of life, the*
> *crown that the Lord has promised to those who love*
> *him* (JAM. 1, 12).

86   TRUSTWORTHY

One of our biggest problems in life is that we don't know what is good for us and we are not yet disposed to let God decide. We are blessed with freedom of action, but we are not quite sure how to use it. So many of us misuse this liberty. We draw up our blueprints, make our plans and then expect almighty God to put his stamp of approval on them and guarantee their success. As if God were some kind of lackey to do our bidding. If things do not work out as we planned, we become frustrated and panicky. The pity is we are not willing to admit that we may not know what is for our good. We think we are so smart. We try to be sophisticated and independent.

Aren't we forgetting that God is still running this world despite all the fumbling attempts of man to mess up his plans? God does have plans for us. He does know what he is doing. Wouldn't it be wise for us to consult with him before we set our mind and heart on our own petty plans?

Perhaps our trouble is that we don't really trust God. We are not truly convinced that he has personal love for and interest in each of us. This borders on blasphemy. There may be times, it is true, when we find it hard to believe that God knows what he is doing in handling our lives . . . when we suffer from the bad will of others . . . when those we love fashion a cross for us . . . when we are burdened with undue anxiety and tension. When we are in a bind like this, our trust in God may be severely strained.

But our trust in God will be severely strained in time of stress only if we have neglected to refer to him all those many other wonderful things that happen in our lives. Only a sick mind or a bitter heart will refuse to acknowledge that there are some wonderful moments in life. If we get into the habit of accepting these wonderful things from the kind hand of God and not usurping the credit, we are building the foundation for truths. If our attitude is correct, we will be able to detect so many manifestations of the concern and care God has for us. These are elements that build up the conviction that God intends nothing but what is good for us. Then when trials come, we are less prone to question the wisdom of God. We don't suddenly lose confidence in the engineer just because we unexpectedly pass through a dark tunnel.

Christ made a valiant attempt to build up our trust in God when he emphasized that God is our Father, with all the love and concern that a good father has toward his children. He even scolded the apostles because of their lack of trust. If you think about it, you will agree that it makes for greater peace of mind to let God in on the ground floor of all our plans.

> *Bow down, then, before the power of God now, and he will raise you up on the appointed day; unload all your worries on to him, since he is looking after you* (1 PET. 5, 6-7).

87   IN GOD WE TRUST

There were two cars in the caravan. In the lead car was Cardinal Mindszenty and his secretary. Following him in the other car were several priests. Suddenly from nowhere, so it seemed, a gang of Communists converged upon the second car. Thinking that the Cardinal was one of the occupants, they began to stone the priests.

Immediately Cardinal Mindszenty realized what was happening. He could easily have driven away, but instead he stopped his car, got out and ran back to the second car, calling "Here I am. I am Mindszenty. Stone me."

This is but one of the little insights into the character of the man whom the Communists not only hate but fear. Given the opportunity the Cardinal could become the rally point overnight for those prisoners behind the Iron Curtain who still possess the dignity of a human being.

What motivates this man of God that he would be willing to expose his life with such apparent abandon? We believe it is a virtue that is too little known and less practiced — the virtue of hope.

Everything we do is done for a purpose and most of the things that we do are done because of the hope of some reward. Power, wealth, glory — these are the things that people of the world hope for and these are the things that drive them to pay the price they are often called upon to pay.

It was the hope of something, or better Someone, that motivated Cardinal Mindszenty to call attention to himself in order to deflect the blows from others and have them heaped upon himself.

He was aware of the promises of Christ; he had the great confidence in these promises. Because he trusted in Christ, he was willing to go to the limit. He would not hold back even if it meant the sacrifice of his life.

Herein lies our lesson. What is the reason why we are so lethargic in the service of Christ and our fellow men, the reason we are remiss in extending ourselves beyond the call of the minimum duty of the spiritual life?

We suggest that the reason is the lack of the virtue of hope. We are not willing to take Christ at his word. We do not trust him enough. We are not willing to throw in our lot completely with Christ because there is some doubt that he will make good his promises. Not so Cardinal Mindszenty; not so the saints. They took Christ at his word and went the limit.

> *These sufferings bring patience, as we know, and patience brings perseverance, and perseverance brings hope, and this hope is not deceptive, because the love of God has been poured into our hearts by the Holy Spirit which has been given us* (ROM. 5, 4-5).

88   TO EACH HIS OWN

"Look alive. You can be replaced by a button!"

There is more fact than fiction in that saying. As the ingenuity of man produces more and more labor-saving devices, he finds himself in acute competition with the very creatures he has called forth. What formerly required many hands to perform can now be performed by one finger pushing a button. The button has become the symbol of our advanced age. If you don't automate, you are out of date.

There is a danger lurking in this symbol, a danger to our spiritual life. Just because everything else is so easy, we expect our sanctity to come just as easily, just as effortlessly. Press a button — instant sanctity. Change the liturgy — instant renewal. There is the danger of looking upon life as some giant vending machine. Drop in a coin, push a plunger and out comes our desired measure of sanctity, neatly packaged. No fuss, no bother.

What we seem to forget is that man is more than material. There is something about the human personality that cannot be weighed and packaged. Man has a spiritual side and it is this side of his personality that must come into play when we speak about sanctity. Sanctity is a person-to-Person relationship that cannot be expressed in a formula, that cannot be imprisoned by material dimensions. This is why sanctity can never be called forth by the push of a button. There are too many elusive elements involved — will, mind, imagination, emotions, circumstances, people, things.

On the part of God there are his infinite perfections, his grace, his respect for the liberty of man. You cannot tie these into a neat little package to be delivered on call.

What we are trying to say, in our stumbling way, is that it is impossible to automate holiness. This must always be hand-made, piecemeal, because each person's holiness is unique. It bears the mark of his individuality. Just as there are no two identical fingerprints, so there are no identical brands of sanctity. Similarity, yes; identity, no.

> *Examine yourselves to make sure you are in the faith;*
> *test yourselves. Do you acknowledge that Jesus Christ*
> *is really in you? If not, you have failed the test* (2 COR.
> 5, 6).

89   SUPER POWER

Behind the giant wheels of industry is a dynamo that generates the power to keep the wheels going. Detached from the source of power, the wheels grind to a halt. How painfully evident this was when the east coast experienced a power failure.

Behind every true Christian is the source of power — Christ. United to Christ we can do wonders. Detached from Christ, our efforts are fruitless. "Without me you can do nothing."

One day a social-minded, non-believing philanthropist, who admired the success and spirit of the nuns who ran the local charity hospital, had plans of erecting a similar institution. He sought the advice of the nuns. Graciously they showed him their plant and explained their procedure. After the inspection tour the nun remarked, "I'm sorry to say it, sir, but I don't think you will succeed."

"And why not?"

"You may imitate our machinery, but you lack the fuel to make it run." She went on to explain to the mystified guest. "The source of our strength and inspiration is Christ in the Blessed Sacrament. It is because of his presence in our chapel that we are able to accomplish what we do."

It is so easy for us to become self-sufficient, relying on our own resources that we scarcely feel the need for the strength that comes from union with Christ. But is this really true? Am I really traveling on my own steam? If the truth were known, it may very well be that we are usurping credit for something that rightfully belongs to Christ.

Sacred Scripture says: "Not that we are sufficient of ourselves to claim anything as coming from us; our sufficiency is from God."

If more of us were aware of Christ as the source of power and consciously relied upon that power, we would have greater success in the business of Christian living. This is a life that requires a source of power that is above human power.

Father, the hour has come: glorify your Son so that your Son may glorify you; and, through the power over all mankind that you have given him, let him give eternal life to all those you have entrusted to him (JN. 17, 1-2).

90   *OUR MISSION*

For years, tons of water gushed over Niagara Falls with enough power to light up the city of New York, but it could not generate a single watt until someone harnessed it. The Texas oil fields have enough fuel to keep our fleet churning the seven seas, but they can't light a single kerosene lamp until someone brings the oil. The sun has enough light for many worlds like this one, but your room will share none of it unless someone draws the shade.

God has seen fit to capsule the remedies for the world's problems in the teaching of his Church, but the world will reap no benefit unless someone brings that message to the world. Look at the mess the world is in today. Is it because the Church has failed? Or is it because we have failed the Church? Do we look upon the fullness of faith as our precious heritage, as our exclusive right?

To possess the truth carries with it the obligation to spread the truth! We cannot carry it around in our pocket as if it belonged to no one except ourselves.

Does this mean that we have to get on a soapbox? Well, no. But then again, yes. Our first obligation is a personal one. We must first of all become so convinced of the truth of our faith that we live it to the hilt. There are to be no half measures here. We have to say to Christ, "Lord, put me down for everything." Only after we have lived the faith fully and tried it unconditionally, will we be fit instruments to fulfill our social obligation.

This social obligation means first of all that we know our faith. We must be equipped to handle it competently in conversation. Just because we know the answers by rote does not say that we are competent to handle the faith in ordinary conversation. We have to be able to start at the level of those with whom we are speaking. We can do this only if we are thoroughly conversant with our faith.

The old bromide, "I never discuss religion," has its origin right here. Religion has become a taboo topic because we have not learned how to handle it dispassionately and intelligently. There is no reason in the world why religion should be shunned as a topic of conversation if we have mastered the art. St. Paul said: "Faith comes by hearing." This is one aspect of our social obligation to bring the truth to the world.

> . . . *always have your answer ready for people who ask you the reason for the hope that you all have. But give it with courtesy and respect and with a clear conscience* . . . (1 PET. 3, 15-16).

91   WORK AND PRAY

One day an old fisherman took a young man across the lake in his boat. The young man was typical of that group of so-called educated individuals, self-centered and self-sufficient. During the short trip the young man noticed that the old man had carved the word "Work" on the one oar and the word "Prayer" on the other. When he saw this, he exclaimed "Uncle, you are out of date. What need is there for prayer if we work?"

The old man did not say a word. Quietly he let go of the oar with the word "Prayer" on it and continued to row with the oar with the word "Work" on it. You can easily picture the result. The boat went around in a circle. There was work, there was expenditure of energy, but there was no definite progress toward the shore.

Thus it is if we rely solely upon our work. Work without prayer is like trying to get to New York on a merry-go-round. We need prayer to give direction to our work. All the work in the world will benefit us not a bit in our effort to arrive at the eternal shore unless it is made a prayer in itself or united with prayer.

If we combine work with prayer, then even the slightest and most insignificant work becomes something big, something that will contribute to our spiritual welfare.

One of the saints said: "Work as if everything depended upon you; pray as if everything depended on God."

This necessity of prayer is based upon our necessity of grace. Without grace it is utterly impossible to make progress in the spiritual life to save our souls.

The ordinary means of grace is prayer. That is why Christ insists that we pray always. We should pray and not grow faint. Our need of grace and therefore our need of prayer is continual.

If the intensity of our spiritual life is in proportion to our fund of grace, it goes without saying that the intensity of our spiritual life is in proportion to our spirit of prayer.

> *I am quite certain that the One who began this good work in you will see that it is finished when the Day of Christ Jesus comes* (PHIL. 1, 6).

92 DAILY INVITATION

The Wise Men appear on the Christmas scene shortly after the birth of Christ. How soon after is not important. What is important is that they do arrive. In this we see a big lesson, namely that the Wise Men were willing to follow an inspiration from on high. We are told that the inspiration took the form of a bright star. Whether there really was a star is not important. Be that as it may, these men accepted the invitation from heaven.

We do not know the agony and anxiety that went into the effort, but in the end we do know they were willing to follow the inspiration. There can be little doubt that this decision cost them dearly. They had to sacrifice the comfort and convenience of home life. They had to part with friends and relatives. They had to face the ridicule of acquaintances who did not see the sense of their action. Because they were willing to respond to grace offered them in this peculiar way, they were rewarded by a vision of Christ.

No day goes by in which we do not receive some inspiration of grace. It may not be as spectacular as that of the Wise Men, but it is an inspiration of grace nonetheless. It may be an impulse to make up with someone. It may be an impulse to lend a helping hand without being asked. It may be an urge to pay a visit to church. It may be the impulse to refuse a date fraught with dangers. It may be an urge to pick up a good book to enrich our spiritual life. It may be any number of similar impulses. These are inspirations of grace. This is how heaven works.

The form in which the inspiration comes is not important. What is important is how much of the spirit of the Wise Men do we possess. How willing are we to respond generously to these inspirations of grace? No doubt, at times our response will cost an effort. We may have to pay by sacrificing comfort and convenience. We may even have to suffer the stigma of going against the stream. But respond we must, if we wish t share the wisdom of the Wise Men.

Our response must be prompt because these inspirations of grace are short-lived. If we dilly-dally, hesitate, seek a way out, they disappear into oblivion, never to return. This is why we have to attune ourselves to recognize the promptings of heaven and respond without delay. For then our response, like that of the Wise Men, will lead to a vision of Christ.

We must never get tired of doing good because if we don't give up the struggle we shall get our harvest

*at the proper time. While we have a chance, we must
do good to all . . .* (GAL. 6, 9-10).

93   *16670*

Charity is like a phrase in a foreign language. It may be
translated in various ways. It may be translated as hot food and
warm clothes, or cheerful care of the sick, or prayers for the dying.
It depends on circumstances. Father Maximillian Kolbe translated
the term in its most challenging meaning.

Taken prisoner during the Nazi invasion of Europe, he was
shipped to the concentration camp of Oswiecim which lies close
to the old German city of Auschwitz. Life in camp was cruel.
In spite of inhuman indignities, Father Maximillian furtively
carried on his priestly work.

In July, 1941, a prisoner had escaped from Block 14, the one
to which Father Maximillian had been assigned. A sickening
feeling clutched the prisoners of that block when they heard this
news. From experience they knew that the penalty for escape
was death for twenty men of the same block, death by slow
starvation. All through the night the men were tortured by the
question, "Will it be I?" The next day the men of Block 14 had
to stand at attention in the broiling sun. Toward evening the
commandant announced, "The fugitive has not been found. In
his place ten of you will die in the starvation cell. The next time
twenty will be condemned."

Then he began to select the ten. At random the condemned were
ordered to step forward. It was a heartless business. Suddenly
one of the victims began to sob in broken sighs, "My poor wife
and children. I will never see them again." Unmoved, the commandant gave the order for the ten hapless men to march. Suddenly a figure stepped from the ranks. Stooped and emaciated,
he walked directly to the Commandant. "Stop," shouted the
officer, "What do you want, you Polish pig?" Softly, so softly,

he could scarcely be heard Father Maximillian said, "I want to die in place of that father of a family. I beg you to accept the offer of my life."

There was a moment of silence. The commandant was so dumbfounded he did not speak. With a gesture he signified his acceptance of the offer. Father Maximillian stepped up to the ranks of the condemned. An assistant coldly jotted down his number — 16670.

This is how one man translated charity.

> *If I give away all I possess, piece by piece, and if I even let them take my body to burn it, but am without love, it will do me no good whatever* (1 Cor. 13, 3).

94   YOURS FOR THE ASKING

How long do you think a person can exist on a starvation diet? A starvation diet is used only in a critical emergency. It is a temporary measure. As soon as a sufficient supply of food is at hand, every sane and sensible person will get off the starvation diet. His common sense tells him that his body must have food in order to continue existence.

If we are so practical in the material realm, why is it that so many are very impractical in the spiritual realm. Why is it that so many are starving themselves to spiritual death when there is food aplenty. Why are so many people going hungry when our Lord has given us a "supersubstantial bread"? If we wonder why there are so many anemic, spineless and spiritless Catholics, I believe the answer is: they are starving themselves.

Surely sometime in our life we must have been impressed by the fact that when Our Lord instituted the Blessed Sacrament he used the form of bread. Bread is a staple daily food. And right there is the significance of it. Just as we need daily bread we need daily Communion.

It is sad to note that the Church had to oblige her faithful to receive Holy Communion at Easter time. What is sad about this legislation is the fact that it had to be enacted. So remiss and so unappreciative had the people become! It is unbelievable that we have to be obliged to take advantage of a privilege.

During the persecution of Catholics during the reign of "Good Queen Bess" in England, a very heavy fine was imposed upon those who were apprehended receiving the sacraments. One nobleman immediately sold his property and turned it into ready cash. He wanted to have money on hand to pay the fine should he be caught. "For the sake of money," he said, "I do not intend to give up my practice of daily Communion."

Because it is so easy for us to go to Communion, we fail to appreciate its true worth. We miss a personal visit from Christ himself; we forego the increase of sanctifying grace; we by-pass the chance for sacramental graces which will help us fulfill our daily duties better; we forfeit the opportunity of having our venial sins remitted and our temptations lessened; we miss a chance for an increase of our glory in heaven.

Fenelon has the right words: "They wish to live for God without living by him. They are dry, feeble, exhausted; they are close to the Fountain of living Water and yet allow themselves to die of thirst."

> *I tell you most solemnly, if you do not eat the flesh of the Son of Man and drink his blood, you will not have life in you. Anyone who does eat my flesh and drink my blood has eternal life and I shall raise him up on the last day* (JN. 6, 53-54).

95   THINK A-HEAD

A few years ago, Fred Snite, the "Iron Lung Kid," died. When he graduated from Notre Dame about fifteen years earlier, he made a trip around the world. One morning in a hotel in China, he awoke to a strange and trying existence. He discovered he could not move. He was stricken with paralysis. He could not carry out those thoughts; he could not execute those plans. He found out, by this sad and terrifying experience, that the head, even though it may be the more noble member of the body, needs the other members.

The head is generally accepted as the source of sensation and direction. It is the head that decrees, plans, and oversees. Without the head, obviously the body could not live. The intentions and designs of the head give color and quality to the actions of the members. The hand may work the very same way to pluck a rose for the altar or pull a trigger to snuff out a rival. The intention of the head makes the difference.

Important as it is, the head in itself is not complete. It depends on the members. If it were not for the legs, how could the head get from place to place? If it were not for the lungs, how could the head speak? The head needs the members.

In a similar way, Christ, the head of the Mystical Body, by reason of his superior power, governs and guides the members of his body. Just as the brain sends impulses along the tiny nerves to the various members directing their activity and enabling them to function properly, so Christ sends the vivifying force of grace to the various members of the Mystical Body. With this grace pulsating through the Mystical Body, the members partake of the life of Christ.

However, as Pope Pius XII wrote, "because Christ the Head holds such an eminent position, one must not think that he does not require the body's help. It is manifestly clear that the faithful need the help of the Divine Redeemer. Yet this too must be held, marvelous though it may appear, Christ requires his members."

If it were not for you and the other members of the Mystical Body, where would Christ find other lips to pray "Our Father"? If it were not for you and other members of the Mystical Body, where would Christ find other hands to bless his children? Where would he find feet to pursue straying sheep? How could he turn the other cheek? How could he give understanding to the misunderstood? Or sympathy to the suffering? How could he counsel the doubtful or instruct the ignorant? You are important! Christ, our head, needs you — the member.

*See *That You May Live* by Cervantes.

> *If we live by the truth and in love, we shall grow in all ways into Christ, who is the head, by whom the whole body is fitted and joined together, every joint adding its own strength, for each separate part to work according to its function. So the body grows until it has built itself up, in love* (EPH. 4, 15-16).

96   DENY YOURSELF*

Anybody entering our civilization would immediately get the impression that our chief concern is creature comforts. Our measure of progress is gadgets, comforts, labor-saving devices. Instinctively we judge a region by television sets, cars, indoor plumbing, washing machines, and the like. There is no premium on moral perfection, mental acumen, artistic production.

There is no question that living for us is easier and a lot of the drudgery has been taken out of work. That life should be made easier would be a good thing if we could prove that it was thereby happier and holier. As far as we are able to observe, this is not the case.

If we are holier, why is there one divorce in three marriages, why has the pornographic business been able to garner millions of dollars annually and contraceptives billions of dollars, why have abortions reached an appalling figure?

If we are happier, why do one in ten land in a mental institution, why do we sell more aspirins, more anacin, more alka seltzer, more pain-killing drugs that induce a mild form of nirvana?

Our quarrel with this cult of creature comforts is that it has landed us in a soft spot. Our cities are crammed with millions of examples of the product of this soft living. All around us we find people with but a rudimentary consciousness, with little moral, religious and esthetic sense.

They satisfy their physiological appetites with no thought of self-denial. They prefer watching games in crowds, afraid they might be alone and discover themselves. They read digests and picture magazines which make no demands on their intelligence. They pander silly prejudices to the detriment of the common good. Except in time of danger or crisis they will not mortify themselves or endure hardship.

From what we know about the Communists, they are tough. The fanatics among them are dedicated and disciplined men who are inured to privation and hardship that will rival the saints. Perhaps one reason why there is less talk about total war is because they believe we will fall into their laps like a soft fruit that has gone rotten at the core. A lot of what they see encourages them in this belief.

If we want to meet the enemy with half a hope of success, we must strengthen our moral fiber. We have to stop pampering our flesh, satisfying our whims, catering to our senses and stultifying our spiritual life. Mortification, self-denial, penance — these are the weapons we need.

---

*See Echoes from Assisi, Liam Brophy, Franciscan Herald Press.

Always wherever we may be, we carry with us in our body the death of Jesus, so that the life of Jesus, too, may always be seen in our body (2 Cor. 4, 10).

97   THE MORNING OFFERING

You and I are here to work for the honor and glory of God. If that is not the aim and intention of our life, we are missing the whole point. I suppose that most of us glibly recite the Morning

Offering and then imagine that from then on everything we do is really done for the honor and glory of God. But is that truly the case? Are we in fact working for the honor and glory of ourselves?

The answers to a few pointed questions will tell us what our real motive is.

What is my attitude toward the particular job that falls to my lot either because of my walk in life or because of some special assignment? If we are working for God and not for ourselves, what we are assigned to do will not make much difference. Once we are satisfied that we are doing the will of God, that is all that matters.

If our intention is correct we will perform any task with zeal and enthusiasm regardless of whether it puts us in the limelight or relegates us to an obscure corner. In other words, the unglamorous hidden task is done just as carefully as the glamorous and obvious one. If we go about a difficult or unromantic assignment with the air of a martyr, we are not working to please God in spite of the Morning Offering.

What is our attitude toward the results we achieve or fail to achieve? If we are overly elated because good results raise our standing in the community, or overly depressed because poor results deflate our ego, for whom are we really working?

God certainly is not upset by results or lack of results. In fact, God does not judge results at all. What he does judge is our motive, our intention. He wants loving service, regardless of results.

When the Apostles returned after a successful mission, they were highly gratified. Christ said to them, "Do not rejoice in this (your accomplishment), but rejoice in this that your names are written in heaven." He is as much as saying, results are not important but the motive behind the job is.

What is my attitude toward the reward or lack of reward? If I am sad and dejected because my work is not noticed, for whom am I working? If I refuse to put forth any effort until I am on the center of the stage, for whom am I working? Thomas a Becket in *Murder in a Cathedral* says:

"The last temptation is the greatest treason,
To do the right thing for the wrong reasons."

Whatever you eat, whatever you drink, whatever you do at all, do it for the glory of God (1 COR. 10, 31).

98   FATHERLY CARE

Life is meaningless unless it is related to God. Everything that touches our lives — creatures, possessions, jobs, friends — have no real value except insofar as they have a bearing on our relationship to God. If they do not clarify or intensify this relationship, they have no lasting value.

What is the basic relationship that we ought to have with God? Christ gives us the answer. It is a startling new relationship that runs throughout the entire New Testament. God is our Father. Christ emphasized the fact that God wants to be known as our Father; he wants to act as our Father; he wants to be accepted as our Father.

Without doubt God is our great Creator, the eternal and just judge, the first and last Cause. But more than anything else God is our Father. Christ removed all doubt when the apostles asked him to teach them how to pray. "When you pray, say 'Our Father, who art in Heaven.' "

In the natural order God is our Father. He is the author of our life. To him we owe everything that we have and everything that we are. Not only do we owe him our existence but the continuation of that existence. If for one moment God would withdraw his fatherly protection, we would fall back into the nothingness whence we came. Without the Providence of God we could not live and move.

More important God is our Father in the supernatural order. When we are reborn to the higher life, we are given a spark of divine life. We begin to share the very life of God himself. We become his children and he becomes our father for the nexus between Father and child in the sharing of life. St. John in his first epistle returns constantly to the thought that we are children of God.

If God is our Father, the first thing we must recognize is that he has authority over us. In thinking of God as Father we may be inclined to regard him in a distorted light. A prevalent misconception is to picture God as an overly-indulgent person very much like a soft-hearted grandfather who will pat us on the head no matter what we do.

God is kind and merciful and forgiving only insofar as these attributes are consonant with his supreme authority. If we are to keep the proper attitude toward God, we cannot forget that Fatherhood bespeaks authority, not softness. God can and does give orders and it is our obligation to accept and obey.

> *Has there ever been any son whose father did not train him? If you were not getting this training, as all of you are then you would not be sons but bastards. Besides we all have our human fathers who punished us, and we respected them for it, we ought to be even more willing to submit ourselves to our spiritual Father, to be given life* (HEB. 12, 8-9).

99   YOU PAINT THE PICTURE

When was the last time we took an honest look at ourselves? It is so easy to get into the habit of thinking that everything is going along just fine; we are riding high and our progress is satisfactory. But the fact is, we may be slipping away from that keen awareness of our destiny as a child of God.

Why don't we get off to some quiet corner and picture in our mind, as vividly as we can, the type of person that we think God would want us to be. Let's fill in the details as specifically as we can. This gives us a good notion of our ideal. Let's fix that firmly in mind. Unless we have a firm picture of an ideal, we are bound to be flabby and flaccid.

Now let's take an honest look at ourselves. The difference between the ideal and the real is startling for most of us. It is precisely that difference that indicates the job that is before us. That difference is our challenge to make the real come as close to the ideal as possible.

The first step is to keep that ideal before our mind's eye. Many people make very little progress in the spiritual life because they do not set their sights on a definite goal. They simply drift with the flow instead of striking out toward a definite specific objective.

Keeping our goal in mind, we have to make systematic efforts to attain it. Wishful thinking will get us nowhere. We have to exert ourselves and at times, we even have to do violence to ourselves. That is the price we have to pay. But anything worthwhile has its price tag. And spiritual progress is worthwhile regardless of the price we are asked to pay.

Besides being systematic, our efforts must be enduring and persevering. To be enthusiastic one day and stop abruptly the next, will accomplish nothing. It is by dint of daily effort, persevering effort, enduring effort that our lives are brought to closer conformity with our ideal.

These are some of the ideas that will come to the fore if we take the time to give our lives an honest scrutiny. Self-knowledge opens vast vistas. The more we know about ourselves the more clearly we see the task ahead of us.

Let me put it like this: if you are guided by the Spirit you will be in no danger of yielding to self-indulgence, since self-indulgence is the opposite of the Spirit (GAL. 5, 16-17).

GOD'S LAW IS OUR LIFE AND LIGHT

100 THE GOOD BOOK

The heart and source of our Christian life is the Gospel. It is a matter of simple logic. If God appeared as man on earth to show us how to love and live, there is only one important thing to do, love and live as we find the God-man doing. The primary source for this information is the Gospel. It is here we see the God-man in action.

Vatican II stresses the point: "This Sacred Synod earnestly and specifically urges all the Christian faithful to learn by frequent reading of the divine Scriptures the 'excelling knowledge of Jesus Christ' (Phil. 3, 8). For ignorance of the Scriptures is ignorance of Christ." To be in step with the Church I must read the Scriptures. Not just sporadically, but regularly.

More than that. If this is the word of God, then I must approach it prayerfully, meditatively. If this is the word of God, then certainly it is one way in which he wants to communicate with me. I have to be open and receptive to any inspiration that may come along. I have to let it speak to me. I have to listen so I can get the message without gloss, without emasculating its spirit, without mitigating its demands, without reducing it to some kind of sweetened anthology for easy-going Christians. This means I have to be back to the Scriptures again and again. Then, hopefully, my judgments, my attitudes, my conduct will be moulded and guided by the spirit of the Gospel.

If I expose myself often enough to the example of Christ who came not to be served but to serve, maybe I will begin to serve by a spontaneous giving of self. In my own way I can bring the Gospel to bear on the circle in which I move. It may not be world-shaking. Few people have the opportunity or talent for that. It may be just a casual encounter of some one in need, a phone call, a visit to a hospital. It may be on a bus, in the elevator, in the office, at home; it may be a warm greeting, a handclasp, a smile. These fall into the same category as the cup of cold water mentioned in the Gospel. Or it may be the rugged fight for fair housing or the effective end of racial discrimination. Whatever it may be, it will represent an effort to relate my daily life to the spirit of the Gospel.

> *Avoid anything in your daily lives that would be unworthy of the Gospel of Christ, so that, whether I come to you and see for myself, or stay at a distance and only hear about you, I shall know that you are unanimous in meeting the attack with firm resistance, united by your love for the faith of the gospel* (PHIL. 3, 27).

101 PATH OF SORROW

So-called popular devotions have been among the fatalities of the liturgical renewal. The reason for this is a misreading of the Constitution on the Liturgy which states expressly: "Popular devotions of the Christian people are warmly commended, provided they accord with the laws and norms of the Church." It goes on to state that where they do not harmonize with the changes they need not be dropped but updated to conform.

Be that as it may, the fact is that the popular devotion of the Way of the Cross has gone by the board and we are the poorer for it.

In its original concept the Way of the Cross was designed to evoke some of the deepest human reactions conducive to man's spiritual growth. First of all, the Way of the Cross engenders a more vivid realization of the fact of the Incarnation and all that that implies because it was only after assuming a human nature was it possible for God to suffer.

Secondly, there is a deeper understanding of the enormity of sin when we contemplate the severity of the price God demanded for reconciliation. Is there an intrinsic necessity for this high cost of reparation? Could God have been satisfied with less? Speculation is academic because the fact is God did not demand less than the suffering of Christ. Dwelling on this suffering, as we do on the Way of the Cross, we are jolted by the realization that sin must be terrible if God demanded this payment.

If we go no further, the Way of the Cross has accomplished a great deal for we do need a deeper penetration into the meaning of sin. In the culture in which we live, we are prone to take sin too lightly. But there is more. Christ was a free agent. In Gethsemane he demonstrated two things — his power to obliterate his enemies and his willingness to freely accept the passion. It is in this willingness that we see the tremendous love Christ has for us. It was only several hours before this incident that he set the norm for ultimate love: "Greater love no one has than this that he be willing to lay down his life for his friend." He chose to be an embodiment of that norm. On the Way of the Cross Christ emerges as the great lover of mankind, willing to give his very life. Can anyone who grasps this fact remain passive? Would there not be a natural urge to respond to this love in some way?

> *If you can have some share in the sufferings of Christ, be glad, because you will enjoy a much greater gladness when his glory is revealed. It is a blessing for you when they insult you for bearing the name of Christ, because it means that you have the Spirit of glory, the Spirit of God resting on you* (1 Pet. 4, 14).

102 WHO CARES?

Run your mind's eye over any great city. In it you will find multitudes living a life in which God has no part, which no ray of faith or hope or true charity illumines. They are born into this great adventure of life, begin their pilgrimage to eternity completely oblivious to higher values and nobler aspirations.

Surely someone is to blame. Surely those of us who are blessed with a clearer vision cannot remain idle spectators of this spiritual chaos in the same helpless way that we view the mad churnings of Niagara Falls.

Either these people have not been taught to know the wonderful heritage of Christ; or if they have been taught they have not been retaught and rewarmed at a stage in their life when they could appreciate its value. What would happen now if they were eagerly sought out? There is a good chance they would be completely different for even the slightest encounter with grace works strange wonders. A sincere interest in them may mean the difference between the salvation or damnation of their souls.

The sad fact remains, we are not seeking them out. We leave them forlornly to the process of action and interaction and reaction with other victims, or what is worse, agents of evil. And we know how thoroughly the process works its mischief.

When disaster strikes in any shape or form, as a nation we can marshal all our forces to relieve the distress. There are no limit to which we can and will go to alleviate physical need. But when it is only souls that are at stake, when there are souls in distress, not even a ripple disturbs our lethargy.

Most people, even good Christians, seem to feel no responsibility for souls. If they do admit a responsibility, they immediately proceed to dilute it by pleading difficulties or exemption or special circumstances. "I have bought five yoke of oxen and am on my way to try them out. Please accept my apologies."

Our approach must not be so scientific that it becomes impractical, nor so indirect that we by-pass our goal nor so gradual that we never reach it. There has to be a straightforward going to soul with a directness of Christ.

---

*See *Souls at Stake* by Ripley.

103 BASIC UNIT

The birth of a child brings into being the basic unit of society, the family. Right there in that family circle a person is to seek his perfection and work out his salvation. It is then of the utmost importance that an individual get off to a good start. Early home life must also be the cradle of the spiritual life.

We are not saying that good home training is foolproof. Where free will is concerned there is no guarantee of a life of virtue. Where a wounded free will is playing a role, the downward pull is greater, and ours is a fallen nature. All the more reason why families should be more concerned about making a good life than making a good living.

To wait until the child is "old enough to make up his own mind" leads to disaster. Unless virtue becomes a part and parcel of early family living, a false standard is apt to arise. If virtuous living is not stressed early in life, what impression will a child get? First impressions, we know, endure. We have to begin, right from the start, to direct the child's mind and heart toward matters that really count.

Some parents imagine their obligations cease as soon as the child is registered in school and attends classes regularly. No institution, no matter how well it functions, can ever supplant the influence of the family. Schools and institutions are mere supplements, not replacements. If training in virtue is neglected in the home, no other agency can repair the loss. On the other hand, a religious training received at the hand of a parent, prudent in effort and fervent in faith is the most important contribution to the individual, the Church and the society. This will last. It will outweigh the influence of associates and the tug of disrupting forces. A virtuous life securely planted in the heart by careful home training can withstand the breath of a thousand frosts. There is much truth in the adage: "As the twig is bent, so the tree is inclined."

> Be shepherds of the flock of God that is entrusted
> to you: watch over it, not simply as a duty but gladly,
> because God wants it, not for sordid money, but

because you are eager to do it. Never be a dictator over any group that is put in your charge, but be an example that the whole flock can follow (1 PET. 5, 2-3).

104 THE WILL THAT COUNTS

Our spiritual life cannot be based upon feeling because feelings are too unstable and unreliable. They come and go. Often they are beyond our control. If we depend upon them to give us a measure of our spiritual growth, we are sure to be frustrated and confused because feelings bob up and down like flotsam.

If one day we feel fervent and joyful in prayer, it may be simply because we had a good dinner and our digestion is normal. If tomorrow we cannot pray and imagine that God has deserted us, it may stem from the simple fact that the chemistry of our body is upset. Such moods of exaltation and depression are often produced by unimpressive agents and have nothing to do with our spiritual life. It may be a wet day, a disappointment in a test, a loss of sleep, a change of daily routine. These can affect our feelings and if we are going to rely upon our feelings to gauge our spiritual life, we might just as well rely upon our blood pressure or body temperature. All this may sound cynical but it is true if we base our spiritual life on feelings.

What really counts is what we will, not what we feel. Our job is to try to control our feelings. When we say we are to control our feelings, we do not mean that we are to stifle or strangle them. We would not be normal if we lost our ability to experience appropriate feeling. Feelings are the standard equipment of the normal person.

Controlling our feelings means to regulate them. When feelings are well tempered, they add beauty to life, they take away monotony, they open avenues of enjoyment that would be closed to us if we were incapable of feeling.

The person who attracts friendships, engenders confidences in time of trial, and in general benefits his fellow man, is the person who registers feeling but in a controlled manner. The person who is going to make lasting progress in the spiritual life is the one who has learned to rule his feelings instead of being ruled by them. He has learned to indulge his feelings under the guidance and influence of the will and intellect. In many instances so much of our religious experiences have been bound up with feeling. For that reason it may be difficult to separate feeling from the spiritual life. But unless we do achieve this separation, our spiritual life is going to suffer by constant fluctuation with the slightest change of feeling. Once we understand that the spiritual life is based upon not what I feel but what I will, we have given it a firm foundation.

> *My prayer is that your love for each other may increase more and more and never stop improving your knowledge and deepening your perception so that you can always recognize what is best* (PHIL. 1, 9).

105   I LOVE YOU

The essential note of love is unselfishness. Love is a relation in which two people look out for the best interest of each other.

Too often the notion of love is identified with the idea of seeking one's own interest. Youngsters think they are in love because of the thrill they get. It is their own interest, their own pleasure that serves as the norm.

Sometimes a girl thinks she is in love with a man, when as a matter of fact she is in love with herself. She loves the way he smoothes her path and soothes her vanity. She loves the smell of the incense he burns before her. In "loving" him she is really sharing his enthusiasm for herself and thus is growing in self-love.

How many fellows think they are in love with a girl because she has the knack of making him feel big. She admires his prowess, his sense of humor, his wit, and his brains. "She has a good head on her shoulders, she appreciates Me. Gee, I must be in love with her." Oh, you big boob, you don't love her any more than you love the man in the moon. You are in love with yourself.

This is the mistake that high school "lovers" make so often. This is why they can say "I love you" to so many people and so often that the words mean hardly more than "Fine weather, isn't it?" This is why they can fall in and out of love a dozen times a season. And mind you, each time they fall in love, it is forever.

If the love is real, it should make both parties better persons. Love is a Godlike act. St. John says, "God is love." If our love is genuine it will take on some of the attributes of God himself. This means it will make us holier, purer, unselfish.

It might help us to read the passage in St. Paul's first letter to the Corinthians; wherein you see the word "charity" you read "love."

"Charity is patient, is kind; charity feels no envy; charity is never perverse or proud, never insolent; does not claim its rights, cannot be provoked, does not brood over injury; takes no pleasure in wrong-doing, but rejoices at the victory of truth; sustains, believes, hopes, endures to the last" (Knox translation).

This points up our ideal of love. A pagan could never appreciate it because he lacks the strength to be utterly unselfish. This is a high ideal which gives some clue what transformation genuine love should effect. Infatuation, sense enchantment, sentimentality, sensuality must be dethroned and true love restored in all its beauty.

Always consider the other person to be better than yourself, so that nobody thinks of his own interest first but everybody thinks of other people's interest instead. In your minds you must be the same as Christ Jesus (PHIL. 2, 4-5).

106   KEEP IN TOUCH

You are not so different as you imagine. So many preen themselves on being an individual apart. They like to think there is something distinctive about them. To a certain extent, this is true. Each of us has an individual personality. Each of us is endowed with a fund of gifts and talents that are peculiarly our own. Each of us has characteristics that single us out from everybody else. We are different.

However, we resemble other people more than we differ from them. We are born in the same manner. We feed on the same type of nourishment. We react, more or less, the same way to medicinal remedies. We are affected, more or less, the same way by disease. We are taught with greater or less success by the same methods. Our reaction to situations and circumstances bear a marked similarity with the reactions of others.

We all have a conscience that tells us right from wrong. If we follow that conscience, our moral life will be pretty much the same as the moral life of others who follow their conscience.

No matter what your problem may be, you are not, thereby, a mild monstrosity or a freak of nature. Some imagine they are so all alone in the daily crises that are typical of our age. They believe that no one else could possibly have problems like theirs. They think their particular problems make them so different they dare not discuss them for fear others will not understand. Once a person understands that he is not that different from the rest of his group, a new vista of hope opens before him. If he is not that different, he will understand that the solutions that helped others can be of help to him. He will not feel forlorn and hopeless.

Because of the basic sameness, we are not to imagine that we are the exception to the rules and regulations that govern the rest of men. So many of the moral and social misfits are individuals who would not accept the fact that the rules that pertain to virtually all human beings, also bind them.

Each individual's problem, under any circumstance seems always more serious and worse, simply because it is his own. This closeness to the problem makes it seem so unique. "Nobody else could possibly suffer like I do." Once we get on this merry-go-round, we are losing touch with reality. You are not so different as you imagine. Keep in touch with the rest of humanity and survive.

If our life in Christ means anything to you, if love can persuade at all, or the Spirit we have in common, or any tenderness and sympathy, then be united in your conviction and united in your love, with a common purpose and common mind (PHIL. 2, 1-2).

107   STANDARDS OF VALUE

The bishops of America in one of their annual statements identified the enemy in these words: "There is an excessive preoccupation with creatures. Materialism has brought about a decline in the influence of religion upon American life. Materialism is the real enemy at home and abroad."

Creatures are to serve as a channel to God, but the way in which so many of us use creatures, they have become clogs and blocks. Instead of serving as a means of getting to God, they have become barriers.

What is the average standard? Do we not measure success by the size of our bankroll, the kind of car we drive, the wardrobe we possess, the television we own? Everywhere we are confronted with a hustle and bustle of activity motivated by the desire to increase material, temporal wealth. This is a day of headaches and ulcers brought on chiefly by our incessant concern about things material. Man will spend his health to gain wealth. Ironically, the circle is completed when man has to spend his wealth to regain his health.

We boast about our high standard of living. What is our essential gauge? Material. If an item cannot be valued in dollars and cents, it is of no value. It is so typical in many families when a new item is introduced, the first question asked is: "How much did it cost?" That one question colors so much of our thinking.

Industry is bent on increasing production in order to increase creature comfort. Again it is material progress that inspires activity. What is wrong with that? Nothing, provided we keep the proper standard of values.

But there is the rub. We have allowed ourselves to become so excessively preoccupied with creatures and creature comforts that our taste for things spiritual has been seriously impaired. We have allowed our standard to get topsy-turvy. We live as if this existence on earth were the be-all and the end-all. We live as if there were no after life. Everything we do, everything we plan, is done and planned as if we were going to continue on earth forever.

That is what we mean by materialism. It is "this-worldness." This materialism, like a deadly cancer, is eating away the moral fiber of our nation. Again we come back to the sore spot. As long as our faith is weak, materialism will grow apace. To combat materialism we must strengthen our faith.

The unspiritual are interested only in what is unspiritual but the spiritual are interested in spiritual things. It is death to limit oneself to what is unspiritual; life and peace can come only with concern for spiritual things (ROM. 8, 5-6).

108   DELICATE BALANCE

The Senate sub-committee investigating the extensive influence of the "Cosa Nostra" has exposed to public view an unusual spokesman. The more one listened to the telecast, the less one was disturbed by what he heard. The underworld spokesman seemed to acquire an aura of respectability. A person almost had to make a double-take to recall that this witness by his own admission was a murderer, double-dealer, extortioner who at one time thrived on all the tricks of gangsterism.

For some strange reason all this immorality was glossed over. Certainly by the witness himself and, I'm afraid, also by many who listened to the testimony. One got the impression that this was a pretty good show. That it was "for real" didn't seem to bother too many. A "so what" callousness emerges.

This is one of the sad developments of our day. A constant exposure to evil dulls our perception of evil.

Christians still believe in sin as one of the greatest misfortunes of life. We still call it by its right name. However, because of the circumstances and the spirit of our times, we are constantly exposed to large chunks of sin. There is the ever-present danger that this continual exposure will blunt our distinction of right and wrong. When a person lives in an atmosphere where there is no sense of sin, his convictions tend to grow dull unless constantly sharpened.

There was a time, for example, when we looked with disapproval at divorce. Now we have become accustomed to it. We seldom register disapproval.

The first time a person commits a serious sin, he is torn by remorse and shame. He hastens to rid himself of his guilt. But should he repeatedly fall into the same sin, he soon blinds himself to its real evil. At first his perception was clear and definite, but continual exposure stifled the voice of his conscience, warped his judgment. A person who continually reads off-color books will lose his taste for more cultured reading. A person who sees nothing but sensual entertainment cannot enjoy a higher form of art.

Perceptions are dulled. Realization is gone. The edge is taken off our awareness. We can help ourselves only by an intense preoccupation with supernatural values to restore the delicate balance.

If after we have been given knowledge of the truth, we should deliberately commit any sins, then there is no longer any sacrifice for them. There will be only the dreadful prospect of punishment . . . (HEB. 10, 26-27).

109 MYSTERY OF THE CROSS

St. Francis of Assisi had a deep and abiding devotion to the Passion of Christ. The flame of love burned strongly in his heart from the time he heard the crucifix speak to him in St. Damian chapel. It was that call that gave direction to his life. As he knelt before that Byzantine crucifix, he begged for the gift of love. And Christ answered his prayer.

Like arrows from a bow, the words of Christ transfixed the heart of Francis. From that time on love became the mainspring of his life. Under the influence of this love all his actions were transformed. As fire penetrates iron, communicating to it its own heat and glow, this love of the Crucified changed the entire being of St. Francis, making it conformable to Christ.

Love can do many things, but one thing love could not do — it could not give Francis the external mark of complete similarity. It was then that Christ himself in the form of a seraph came to the aid of love and impressed on the hands and feet and side of Francis the scars of our Redemption. We must understand that the secret of Mount Alverno, where the stigmatization took place, was not the pain of the wounding but the love that prepared Francis for those wounds.

This is the very same secret of Christ's wounding on the heights of Calvary. The mystery of the cross is not pain and suffering, but love. Suffering is merely the manifestation of love. Christ did not love suffering for its own sake. This is evident from the Garden of Gethsemane where he recoiled from the prospect of his coming ordeal. "Father, let this chalice pass from me." He tells us why he underwent the suffering: "That the world may know that I love the Father and as the Father has given commandment, so do I."

In a similar manner the saints are not morbid when they embrace suffering, self-denial, and mortification. They do not love these for their own sake, because suffering in itself is not good. A toothache does not automatically make a man better. It may even make him surly and hard to live with. The point is, the saints loved Christ and because they loved Christ they were willing to accept suffering.

Today there are few lovers of the cross because we fail to understand its secret — love! Even in this life earthly love gilds suffering and removes its sting. If there was more love, there would be less shirking the cross. St. Francis de Sales says: "Suffering borne for the love of God participates in the qualities of its source (which is God). To think of Calvary except in terms of love is a perversion.

But to meditate on the suffering of Christ within the context of love will produce in our lives a generosity and strength in doing good which will endure because it is a sharing in the selfless love of Christ which is stronger than suffering, stronger even than death.

As for me, the only thing I can boast about is the cross of our Lord Jesus Christ, through whom the world is crucified to me, and I to the world (GAL. 6, 14).

110   LOUIS PASTEUR

When you opened the carton of milk this morning, you were confident that it was one of the safest and purest foods to reach your table. The reason why milk is free from germs is because of the work of Louis Pasteur. He is the great French scientist who developed the method of pasteurizing milk in order to free it from dangerous bacteria and germs. This is but one in the long list of contributions that Louis Pasteur has made to humanity.

Behind all these discoveries is a great man from whom we can learn many a lesson. Pasteur learned something more important than how to conquer germs that may ravage the body. He knew how to prevent the germs of sin from taking their toll of spiritual life.

In his day many a scientist looked at the poor dead flesh beneath the microscope and said: "This is all there is. There is nothing more." But Pasteur could look beyond the microscope and cry, "There is more, much more. There is God."

Because he looked for more in life than meets the naked eye, he was able to discover the process of Pasteurization. In his own living he looked beyond what meets the senses and found the richness of the spiritual life in God.

Just as regularly as pasteurized milk is at our door in the morning, Louis Pasteur was found at the church door. Not a day passed in which he did not feed on the Bread of Life. In his battle against germs he stripped away sentimentality, illusion, and ignorance.

This attitude he carried into his personal life and found God at a time when it was not popular to acknowledge God. One of the few Catholics to be admitted to the French Academy, he was a credit to his faith in every respect. He made bold to tell the members of the Academy, "Do not let yourselves be tainted by a barren scepticism." And this at a time when scepticism was the fashion. On another occasion he said, "Gentlemen, you would not hesitate to admit the existence of God, if your hearts and your lives were right."

Louis Pasteur was a great man in many respects. He is greater by far in his relations with God. He is a graphic example of a man who can be truly intellectual, a progressive scientist and a firm believer in God.

> *You see, God's grace has been revealed, and it has made salvation possible for the whole human race and taught us that what we have to do is give up everything that does not lead to God, and all our worldly ambitions; we must be self-restrained and live good and religious lives here in this present world* (TIT. 2, 11-13).

111 FRIENDSHIP

No man is an island. There is a basic need in all of us to relate to other people. It is possible to go through life without close relatives. But for a person to lead a half-way normal and satisfying life, he must have friends. This is the way we are made. We are born with a certain incompleteness and the anti-social, anti-people character is not normal.

Friendships, however, do not occur automatically. Nor do they continue automatically. Like fences, friendships must be kept in constant repair. There must be a mutual endeavor to keep the friendship alive. This is a two-way street. Nothing atrophies more quickly than unrequited friendship.

Friendships are necessary and precious and ought to be cultivated. They fill a human need.

A true friend is a protection for virtue, a strong defense. There
are times in our lives when we must open our hearts to an intimate confidant. We need an equal in whose presence we can
speak with perfect freedom, in whose presence we can dare to
be ourselves, let our hair down without fear of recrimination.
If we do not have such a friend there is danger of speaking out
of turn to our detriment or putting our trust in someone who may
betray it.

A true friend is a sympathetic counselor to whom we are willing to bring our doubts and difficulties. With his help we can
hope to arrive at a satisfactory solution. He will be someone who is
devoted enough not to hesitate to tell us the truth. He will not
dissimulate or mislead because he loves us and wants to save
us from acts of imprudence.

A true friend is a comforter who is willing to listen to our
turbulent tale of woe with unending patience even though he
may have heard it a hundred times before. Somehow he will find
the right word to encourage and console. Sometimes just being
there is sufficient.

Scripture assures us that "a faithful friend is a strong defense
and he that hath found one hath found a treasure. A faithful
friend is the medicine of life and immortality."

These are benefits we expect and accept from our friendships.
These are the benefits our friends have a right to expect from
us. It works both ways. There must be a give and take. It is not
fair to drain the cup of friendship and not give of ourselves to
replenish the supply.

*Fragrant oil gladdens the heart, friendship's sweetness
comforts the soul. Better a friend near than a brother
far off* (PROV. 27, 9-10).

112   GET THE FACTS

One of the effective ways to temper an emotion is by refraining from giving external expression to it. It is a common experience that feelings are intensified when they are translated into actions. If a person gives in to his feelings of depression by assuming a moping posture, speaking in a doleful voice with the proper sighs, he is bound to intensify his depression. Should he assume an external air of cheerfulness, his depression will be greatly mitigated.

An angry man who gives vent to his feelings of irritation can easily work himself into a fury. On the other hand if he voluntarily suppresses the physical signs of wrath, the emotion will remain within reasonable limits. There is a great deal of practical sense in counting to ten before allowing ourselves to act in anger.

Another aid to emotional control is "get the facts." If a person gives in to worries or fear frequently, let him get to the facts behind the worry or fear. Let him face up to the fact that the fear or worry is futile. Neither will help the situation.

One of the causes for feelings of depression and even worry is the fact that we are too concerned about what others think about us. It is folly to let our peace of mind depend on circumstances that are beyond our control. It is well and good to act in a way that will merit the good opinion of others, but it is foolish to become despondent, irritable, impatient if that good opinion is not forthcoming.

The opinions other people have about our behavior are colored by personal bias. Over that we have no control. But we do have control over our own reaction to their opinions. If our conscience is clear, what difference should it make if we are blamed or praised?

If we are in a situation that rubs us the wrong way and causes outbursts of emotion, it is healthy and sane to take a sensible attitude toward the situation. If we can change the situation, let's change it. If we cannot change the situation, we learn to live with it. There is no point in concentrating on those aspects of it that get on our nerves. There is always a bright side, if only we take the pains to find it.

You will always have your trials but, when they come, try to treat them as a happy privilege; you understand that your faith is only put to a test to make you patient, but patience too is to have its practical results so that you will become fully-developed, complete, with nothing missing (JAM. 1, 2-4).

113   CREEPING CANCER

Worldliness is insidious. It is like a polluted atmosphere that penetrates everywhere and carries infection into every crack and crevice. Few succeed in escaping its harmful effects. Living as we are in an environment that is saturated with this worldly spirit all of us are more or less tainted by it.

Opposed to the spirit of the world is the spirit of asceticism which aims at overcoming the unwholesome tendencies inherent in our weakened nature. Asceticism faces toward the supernatural and eternal, and as such, will make no compromise with the spirit of the world.

It is the all-important task of every Christian to preach asceticism and live it. As Christians, we are declared enemies of worldliness. It is our avowed purpose to combat it relentlessly and consistently. If we fall in with the ways of the world, accept its ideals, and are guided by its principles, we are not true to our calling. We are betraying one of the most vital interests entrusted to our care.

It is no secret that asceticism is not popular in our day. We seem to forget that Christianity is essentially an ascetical religion. Christianity without asceticism is like a body without a heart. The less we are convinced of this, the more we are infected with the spirit of the world.

The fundamental tendencies of our times are basically pagan for they tend to exalt the things of this world. To the pagan this world is everything; to the Christian it is to be mortified. Which of these two views has the upper hand at the moment is not difficult to see when we observe the cult of the flesh in evidence in sports, in fashions, in comforts, and in luxuries. It is belaboring the obvious to say that we need a revival of the spirit of asceticism.

This revival of asceticism can be effected in a telling manner by popularizing the ideals of St. Francis of Assisi who is everybody's saint. Few saints had the impact on human events that St. Francis had. At a time when the world was growing cold in its love for Christ, it was St. Francis who, almost singlehandedly, brought the world back to Christ and Christ back to the world. The asceticism that he practiced is characterized by the gentleness and charm of the spirit of Christ. It is the type of asceticism that finds favor today.

> *You must not love this passing world or anything that is in the world. The love of the Father cannot be in any man who loves the world, because nothing the world has to offer — the sensual body, the lustful eye, pride in possessions — could ever come from the Father but only from the world; and the world, with all it craves for, is coming to an end* (1 Jn. 2, 15-16).

114   THE SOLID ROCK*

Standing on the swastikaed stage in the glare of teeming floodlights in Berlin, Adolph Hitler solemnly announced to the 60,000 Nazi Socialists and to the world: "I promise you that if I so wished, I would destroy the Church in a few years. It is hollow and false and rotten through and through. One push and the whole structure would collapse. Its day is done."

History testifies that Hitler never made a bigger mistake. With hobnailed goosestep he managed to trod roughshod across the bruised body of Europe. We can understand that mistake. But why should he try to stub his toe on the Rock of Ages? Men more powerful than Hitler have broken their necks in that way. Men more clever than he have tried to snuff out the life of the Church, but she stands unharmed and sings the *Dies Irae* over their remains.

The world-conquering caesars tried to strangle it as a Babe. Arius tried to take away Christ by denying he was true God. Mohammed tried to enslave the Church by the sword. Innovators tried to prove that the "gates of hell" prevailed against her. Down through the ages her enemies snarled with Voltaire, "Crush the infamous thing." But the Church lives and thrives. We are secure; we have no worry. We exult in opposition; we progress in adversity. We thrive under blows. Day after day we experience the truth of the words: "Thou art Peter and upon this rock I will build my Church and the gates of hell will not prevail against her." If the gates of hell will not prevail against her, surely nothing less than the gates of hell will ever prevail against her.

Did you ever stop to realize why the gates of hell would not prevail against her? The reason is because the Church is not just another organization like a group of people coming together to honor a great man. It is not a mutual aid society like a life insurance company. The Church is not an organization like a club. It is an organism. It is like the human body that grows and develops and increases from within. It is not formed by men coming together to honor Christ; it is formed rather by the life of Christ flowing into men.

Christ was continually talking about this life. "I have come that you may have life and have it more abundantly." "I am the vine; you are the branches. Abide in me and I in you. As the branch cannot bear fruit of itself unless it remains on the vine, so neither can you unless you abide in me." That is the life that Christ came to give us. A participation in his own divine life. With this life coursing through the Church, she cannot decay. She is just as vigorous as she was the day she was founded.

*See *That You May Live* by Cervantes.

115   LIVE IT UP

Okay! So we ask you to become a saint. Don't look at me as if I have asked you to grow a second head. I know I can call you anything from cutie to snooty but I must not call you a saint. All I have to do is tell you your religion is showing and you begin to fidget and squirm and blush in an uncomfortable manner. What gives? Do you think sanctity makes you some kind of freak? Do you think sanctity means you have to put some skin on moldy bones.

If that is what you are thinking, you are standing on your head. Stand up straight and look around for a clear day you can see to eternity. And that is what sanctity is all about. Looking to eternity. Like it or not that is where you are headed. Sanctity means using the shreds of eternity which we call time in such a way that you will be pleased, your neighbor will be pleased and God will be pleased. So what's your beef?

Saints are not buried in monasteries; they do not live in the clouds. They are men and women so many feet tall, so many years old, so many pounds heavy. They lived yesterday; they live today. They lived in Rome, they live in Chicago. But they were human beings who took Christ seriously when he said, "You are to be perfect as your heavenly Father is perfect."

Big order? Granted. But are you afraid of a challenge? The job becomes a bit easier when we recall that Christ became one of us to show us how to live. But even this example is darkened and glossed over that it is hardly recognizable. So what happens. Just about the time when the picture fades, along comes a person who lives before our very eyes the life of Christ, proving once again that it is possible. It is not the great deeds they performed nor the books they wrote that is so important. It was their continual "love-in" with God that makes the saint a dynamic figure. Because of the saint, the likeness to Christ makes them virile, strong and forceful. In comparison, others are shabby and weak-kneed.

So you take a look at yourself. What do you find? Sin and sinful tendencies, foibles and follies, tricks and quirks of an enfeebled nature. We are push-overs for unwholesome desires. Is this the stuff of which saints are made?

Let's face it. It is! But not by yourself. The transforming element is grace. Grace will take you as you are with your temper, your shyness, your stupidity, your intelligence, your dances, your dates, your temptations. Given half a chance, grace will elevate, ennoble and refine. Gently, imperceptibly, it can make something wonderful out of a petty, earth-clinging soul.

However, it is not automatic. There is the rub. Man's free will enters the picture. There has to be active, personal cooperation. Grace will not force us, but if we lend ourselves more and more to the transforming power of grace, we will be pleasantly surprised and richly rewarded.

> *Astonishment seized them and they were all saying to one another, 'What teaching! He gives orders to unclean spirits with authority and power and they come out* (LK. 4, 36).

116   STEP LIGHTLY

"I can't do anything right!" How many times have you said that to yourself? Do you feel that you are doomed to failure every time you attempt something? Does this feeling make you sit on your hands and not even try? These are indications that you lack confidence in yourself. There are several things that you can do about it.

Be honest about yourself and recognize that no matter how miserable you feel about yourself there are some good points. You must recognize and admit that like everybody else you do have some talents, gifts and abilities. If you deny this, you are just plain dishonest. Besides that, you are ungrateful to God. Your gifts and talents may not be as great or manifold as you would like, but the fact is you do have some. Don't sit around bemoaning what you lack, but get busy and develop what you do have. Whether you have much or little, put it to work.

Having admitted your gifts, you must also realize that you are still a member of the human race and therefore there are limitations to what you can do — this is no reason for saying you can't do anything. It is simply the admission of a dependent, limited being. So what? That is the way all of us are made.

The person who lacks self-confidence wants everything guaranteed before he will make a step. This is stupid. If everybody acted on that principle, nothing would ever get done. We have to learn to take just one step at a time. We can see just so far, even if it is a short distance. That is the step we take.

When you drive a car at night, it is foolish to drive so fast that you could not control your car beyond the limits of your headlight beam. It is sensible to stay within those limits, but you don't stop driving just because you can't see beyond. As you progress, the light beam shows more. As you take one step in life, you see where to take the next step.

Don't expect to be perfect. Just because you have failed once, does not make you a failure. Expect to make mistakes. That is why we have erasers on pencils. But why dwell on these mistakes? Is that sensible? If you fall flat on your face, do you just lie there? No! You pick yourself up and start anew.

Never give in then, my dear brothers, never admit defeat: keep on working at the Lord's work always, knowing that, in the Lord, you cannot be laboring in vain (1 Cor. 15, 58).

117   LITERARY DIET

Recently a local newspaper featured an interesting series of articles on reading. Laymen were asked to comment on some book that affected their lives. It is surprising how deep and far-reaching this effect is at times. With some it even meant a right-about-face.

Good reading has the same effect on a person's character as association with wise and noble companions. We are often inspired by the mere presence of a sterling character. The desire to imitate is often impelling. In good reading we come in close contact with the noble, good and true. The good ideas thus encountered often become the mainspring of good deeds; the feelings and emotions experienced strike a sympathetic chord and attune the heart to lofty ideals. Just as a piece of linen kept in a perfumed casket takes on the delicate fragrance, so a young person's character is sweetened and strengthened by reading. This is especially true of books that depict the lives of high-principled men and women, for in such we see the very embodiment of high ideals.

Our printing presses are churning out millions upon millions of copies of reading matter. Magazines, books, paperbacks — who can even estimate how many readers are reached daily? Good and bad, classic and trash, moral and immoral — the printing presses keep turning. Literacy in America is paying off in dollars and cents. But is it paying off in morality and spiritual sense? That is the big question we ought to ask ourselves. We would like to think that it is paying off for the good of society, but we are afraid the fact is otherwise.

We know that there are two worlds constantly struggling for our attention, service and love. The one belongs to time and is concerned about the pleasures of this life. The other belongs to eternity and is concerned about our soul and God. Both are using the press to attract the attention of the people. Who has the edge? The next time you pass a magazine rack, scan the contents and see who is flooding the market. That is the thing we are up against. We have to fight through a mess of inane, useless, and downright vicious material to get at something decent. If the mind becomes cluttered with the trash there is no room for Godly ideals.

The time is sure to come when far from being content with sound teaching, people will be avid for the latest novelty and collect themselves a whole series of teachers according to their own tastes; and then, instead of listening to truth, they will turn to myths (2 Tim. 4, 3).

118   BE MERCIFUL

"Once a thief, always a thief." That seems to be the philosophy of too many people in the world. They are like a pack of wolves hot on the trail of a tiring deer. Let the deer but stumble or run into a blind ravine, and the pack is upon it tearing it apart.

Let a pack of human wolves learn about the failings and sins of others and they proceed to tear his character to shreds. In many instances it makes little difference whether the failings and sins are real or alleged. Just so it is something to work on. It is so hard for the fallen to work their way back into the good grace of society because of the jungle tactics of the neopagans.

Fortunately, man's ways are not the ways of God. On May 8, 1902, the volcanic mountain, Mt. Pelee, on the island of Martinique blew its head off. Suddenly as if some giant knife had made an incision in the belly of the mountain, its sides burst open. With incredible speed a cloud of lava and steam and deadly dust suffocated the city, taking the lives of 40,000 inhabitants.

The only person spared was a solitary Negro chained to a post in an underground dungeon. He was found days later badly burned but still alive. God had spared the only person whom the rest had branded as a criminal least worthy of living. Of all the people on that island God had selected as an object of his special love and care a despised criminal. Here is the mercy of God in action.

Mercy is a practical sympathy and compassion for the misery of another. It implies a sincere effort to remove or at least alleviate the misery. This perfection God has in the highest degree. He is the "Father of mercies and God of all consolation."

The greatest misery is that kind whose effect is most terrible and enduring. Sin falls in that category. Sin is the greatest misery that can befall a person. It is precisely here that the mercy of God is manifested most clearly. If there is anything that God wants us to understand, he wants us to understand that he is merciful.

"Let the wicked forsake his ways and the unjust man his thoughts and let him return to the Lord and he will have mercy on him." "I desire not the death of a sinner but that he be converted and live." God's mercy is revealed above all in the Incarnation. He sent his only Son to redeem man from the misery of sin.

In a day that is marked with pessimism and hopelessness we have to emphasize more than ever that God's ways are not like the ways of man. He stands with open arms to welcome the sinner who wants to work his way back into his good graces.

If mercy has been shown to me, it is because Jesus Christ meant to make me the greatest evidence of his inexhaustible patience for all the other people who would later have to trust in him to come to eternal life (1 Tim. 1, 16b).

119   SET VALUES

If we want to make a success of life we have to maintain a correct standard of values. This is true in any phase of living, but it is especially true of our spiritual life. Just as soon as our sense of values becomes distorted, we can be sure our life will reflect that distortion. For that reason it is important that we keep certain basic principles clearly in mind.

Whenever we are tempted to commit sin, we ought to recall what St. Francis once wrote: "brief is the pleasure, eternal the penalty." Temptation always presents evil under some aspect of good. We never go for evil as evil. It is always sugarcoated. The aspect of good is generally spurious and fictitious, usually some kind of pleasure — mental, emotional, physical. But no matter how intense the pleasure may be it must always come to an end.

Then the reaction sets in — disappointment and remorse. Even if a person spends a whole lifetime in sinful pleasure, he will learn that that too must come to an end. No matter how long we live, life is too short. After the sinful pleasure, eternal remorse sets in.

We have to be on our guard constantly lest we be duped by the devil. We have to learn to see through his ruses and understand that no matter how the odds stack up it is always a bad bet to trifle with temptation. It is so easy for us to rationalize our giving in to temptation. The bait is so alluring. A little foresight and a little hindsight will keep us on the alert.

It is not enough, however, merely to avoid sin. We are expected positively to practice virtue, to accept the sufferings and trials that come our way. This is not an easy task, but here again we must keep our perspective.

St. Paul writes: the sufferings of the present time are not worthy to be compared with the glory to come. If we view the whole picture in the light of eternity, then suffering is slight. The suffering we put up with in resisting temptations, the suffering we put up with in practicing virtue will pay rich dividends in measureless glory.

It comes down to this: What are our standards for gauging the value of those things that make up our daily life?

It was by faith that, when he grew to manhood, Moses refused to be known as the son of Pharoah's daughter and chose to be ill-treated in company with God's people rather than enjoy for a time the pleasures of sin (HEB. 11, 25).

120   *LOST AND FOUND*

The more I deal with high school and college students in counselling and retreat work, the more I hear the troubled complaint, "Father, I don't feel close to God. I seem to have lost him and don't know where I can find him." This seems to be one of the stages in the growing-up process. What is happening is this: we are maturing. In many areas we are rising above the "feeling" world, but in religion we are reluctant to leave the security we once knew when we felt God was so close to us. We haven't quite given up the idea that God is something we can enjoy like a milk shake. We are still trying to find God by squeezing our emotions. And if these things do not work, we panic. We imagine we have lost God.

Finding God is a matter of intelligence and faith. We find God not by jacking up our feeling, but by using our intelligence and opening our eyes of faith. We can find God in his handiwork. All of God's creation portrays the touch of an artist — the crimson glory of the sunset, the symmetry of a snowdrop, the perfume of the lilacs in spring, the music of a child's laughter. Our intelligence can find God here.

Our faith can find God within ourselves. "Do you not know," says St. Paul, "that you are temples of God?" Our faith can find the Image of God in the needy family down the street, in the classmate across the aisle, in the fellow-worker, in the members of our family. "What you do to the least, you do to *me*." Each of these certainly is a potential reminder of the Creator.

We need not be afraid to grow up. We need not be afraid to ignore our feelings. We have to be bold enough to use our intelligence, and daring enough to let our faith guide us. We worry too much about having lost God. The mere fact that we are concerned is a sure sign that we have not lost him. When we no longer seek him, when we are no longer concerned about possessing him, then we are in real trouble. So the passing anxiety about the absence of God may be a sign of growing up. We are beginning to look at God from a different perspective and we are not quite accustomed to the sight.

Now it is impossible to please God without faith, since anyone who comes to him must believe that he exists and rewards those who try to find him (HEB. 11, 6).

121 HE AIN'T HEAVY

The burden was obviously too heavy for her meager strength, but she insisted and carried the boy across the street. "Isn't he too heavy for you?" asked a passer-by.

"Nah," came the reply, "he ain't heavy. He's my brother."

If only that sentiment were put into practice in every family. A great deal of the unhappiness in family life comes from a lack of consideration for those near and dear to us. Why is it that the chance visitor receives the friendly bright smiles, the pleasant words and constant attention? Why are we affability personified when there is a guest in the house, but when there is nobody around except the family we show the churlish side of our character? Our own are just as deserving of love and care, thoughtfulness and consideration as the casual acquaintance. Those who share our household deserve more forbearance than we are wont to give.

The trouble may be that our constant experience of their failings and shortcomings tend toward exaggeration. If we dwell on these irritating qualities in a less emotional state, we will be amazed how they shrink to their true proportions. The trouble is we let our imagination take hold of the insignificant incidents and paint them in the most lurid colors. By the time we have finished, they have grown out of proportion to their true value.

It helps to strive for a certain flexibility. No one's character is so hardened that it cannot be adjusted. Adaptability is a sign of maturity. After living with someone for a while we certainly become keenly aware of their peculiarities. There may be a lot of things, insignificant in themselves, to which members of our family attach a great deal of importance. To ride roughshod over these in a thoughtless, overbearing way does not make for happiness in the family circle. Is tolerance too high a price to pay for family peace?

On the other side of the ledger, how much do our own peculiarities strain the tolerance of others. Tit for tat. They put up with me, I put up with them. Every home certainly wants to be a happy home. To achieve this, each individual must contribute his share. The love and concern we have for each other should not be like a submarine that comes to the surface only when there is trouble. It has to be an every-day affair.

> *May the Lord be generous in increasing your love and make you love one another and the whole human race as much as we love you. And may he so confirm your hearts in holiness that you may be blameless in the sight of our God* (1 THES. 3, 12-13).

122 LIFE'S POISON

Do you know how to bear a grudge?

The first step is to learn what a grudge is. It is that prolonged resentment we feel toward someone for a real or imaginary slight or offense of which we have been the victim. It eats away at our judgment about the perpetrator of the deed.

I doubt that children know how to hold a grudge. They merely pout a bit and show their resentment in some disagreeable but not too serious manner.

With an adult it is different. If he wants to hold a grudge, he must strive to make his pouting a little more dignified and righteous. It takes only a little practice. For example, try a cold, disdainful silence. This is sure to wither a person. Ignore any questions put to you. If you can't avoid an answer, make sure it comes out in monosyllabic grunts. What we are striving for is to freeze out the party who hurt us. The best way to keep aloof from any plans or activities in which he is interested is simply not to engage in any conversation. You have to be careful not to let him trap you.

But you can't observe silence forever. So when you have to speak, try sarcasm. Those biting comments and caustic interpretations fit in neatly, because everything that person says or does is suspect. After all, look what he did to you. Of course, you are justified. Anybody who has hurt you is incapable of any decency. He should be exposed.

For variety try sadness. You know what I mean: let your shoulders sag, your lips drop as you cultivate that woe-begone look. Let the whole world hear you say in so many words: "See what he has done to me. Poor me. Don't you see how I suffer." That is a subtle way to hold a grudge. Keep it up long enough and you'll get back at him.

Don't give up too soon, because the longer the grudge lasts, the more firm it becomes. This is exactly what you want — perpetuate it as long as possible.

It helps to be touchy or sensitive so you can quickly detect when you are slighted. You can't be too naive about it otherwise you will never catch on. You have to be smart so no one pulls the wool over your eyes.

With a little experience you can become the best grudge bearer in the world. Good luck.

Never repay evil with evil but let everyone see that you are interested only in the highest ideals. Do all

> *you can to live at peace with everyone. Never try to get revenge; leave that, my friends, to God's anger* (Rom. 12, 17-18).

123   HEART-TO-HEART

If prayer is the mere perfunctory recitation of a formula, why should we not go modern and make a recording and let the machine do our praying for us? Why not do as the lazy chap did? He went to the bother of copying the Our Father on a piece of paper and tucked it under his pillow. At night he would jump into bed and say: "Lord, you know my sentiments; they are under my pillow."

But that won't do at all, for we realize that prayer is not mere lip service. It must come from the heart and not from the teeth. It is from deep down inside. It is a heart-to-heart talk with God.

Conversation with God! Have you ever given thought to what that means?

A few years ago, while in Rome, I had a chance to be present for an audience with the late Holy Father. That visit will go down as one of my treasured memories. I think it was a great privilege. Yet what is an audience with the Pope compared to a heart-to-heart talk with Almighty God every time I pray? With all his dignity, authority, power and majesty the Pope is still a human being, a creature of God. If we consider it so great a privilege to speak with him, how much greater is the privilege to speak with God, the infinitely perfect God? Have you ever thought of prayer as a privilege?

Prayer is one of the most noble acts of which man is capable. If we realize this fact we would not look upon prayer as a burden;

we would not find prayer irksome and tiresome. We would be anxious and eager to pray.

Perhaps our trouble is we fail to grasp the nobility and sublimity of prayer, because we do not comprehend the creature-Creator relationship. We lose sight of the fact that as a creature we are so totally dependent upon God that if for one moment he would withdraw his conserving power over us, we would fall back into nothing whence we came. It is almost a hopeless task to think of ourself as nothing. On the other side there is God, the great God, the mighty, infinite God who is all perfections in their highest possible degree. It is an impossible task to think of God as he is. But just pause a moment to let some idea of the tremendous gap between us and God take hold of us.

To think that this great God will listen to our puny voice! To think that this insignificant nothing occupying an obscure corner in this world can address God! When we begin to understand some of the implications of these words, then we begin to understand something of the dignity and nobility of prayer.

> *In your prayers do not babble as the pagans do, for they think that by using many words they will make themselves heard. Do not be like them; your Father knows what you need before you ask him. So you should pray like this: Our Father, etc.* (Mt. 6, 7-9).

124   TRUE WISDOM

At times we are stunned by the impact a handful of radicals can have at an open meeting. This influence can be explained in part by the desperation that drives most fanatics. It can also be explained in part by the fact that this hard core group can articulate its stand. They know what they stand for. They do not hesitate to make it their business to know. This knowledge begets confidence and confidence begets strength.

Can we say the same for the Christian? Does he know how to face the fact; how to probe the roots of a question; how to gauge matters by an objective norm? What is distressing is that so many are not even interested in learning. Oh, we can cram our craniums with a fund of assorted fact to be glibly rehearsed at the behest of a teacher, but is that learning?

Real learning will equip a person to heed the warning of St. Paul: "Make sure that no one traps you and deprives you of your freedom by some secondhand, empty, rational philosophy based on the principles of this world instead of on Christ."

There are several evils in particular we ought to shun. Culpable ignorance which does not see the will of God because it does not want to see. If a person does not want to learn, you cannot reshape his stance no matter how hard you try. There is a certain snugness about this person that cannot be penetrated. The pity is that because he wants his ignorance he also wants all the stupidity that goes with it. What can you do with such a person? He has to want to help himself before anyone else can be of service.

Another evil is illusion. We are constantly nurturing our illusions. We live in illusion and unfortunately so many of us die in our illusion. We are so used to viewing life through the glasses of illusion that everything is judged in a way that caters to our whims. Before we ask what does God want, we take counsel with our self-interest. So loud and insistent is the clamor of illusory self-interest that it drowns out the voice of God.

Not so bad, but bad enough is the ignorance begotten of frivolity and distraction. People hampered by this kind of ignorance are so taken up with trivialities that they cannot give serious thought to important matters. This is the jitterbug, jack-rabbit type. A former professor had the right word when he called them "whiffle-minded." The result is they know nothing real about themselves, where they are going, much less how to get there.

Finally there is the ignorance that is the natural consequence of the fall of man which has darkened our intellect. It is not our fault; still it is there and we have to recognize and deal with it.

In any of these cases we have to be brutally honest with ourselves to determine the state and degree of our ignorance. Only then is there any hope of helping ourselves.

> *He is the image of the unseen God and the first-born of all creation, for in him were created all things in heaven and on earth . . . all things were created through him and for him* (COL. 1, 15-16).

125   MONEY'S NOT EVERYTHING*

Money is not everything. We spend our health gaining wealth and then have to spend our wealth to regain our health. For the person who thinks money is everything there is a rude awakening. The odds are stacked against him.

In 1923, eight of the most successful business men in the United States held a meeting in a hotel in a midwestern city. Among them were the president of the largest independent steel company, the president of the largest utilities company, president of the largest gas company, the greatest wheat speculator, the president of the New York Stock Exchange, a member of the U. S. President's cabinet, the greatest "bear" on Wall Street and the president of the Bank of International Settlements.

In this group was concentrated so much wealth that the imagination staggers. One would think that these gentlemen who were lionized as the epitome of success "had it made."

Twenty-five years later the world's most successful and wealthy businessmen had the following record:

The president of the largest independent steel company, Charles Schwab, died a bankrupt. He lived on borrowed money the last five years of his life.

The president of the largest public utilities company, Samuel Insull, died penniless in a foreign country where he had fled.

The president of the largest gas company, Howard Hopson, was hopelessly insane.

The greatest speculator of wheat, Arthur Cutten, died abroad insolvent.

The president of the New York Stock Exchange, Richard Whitney, had recently been released from Sing Sing.

The member of the President's cabinet, Albert Fall, who was involved in the Teapot Dome scandal, was released from prison so he could die at home.

The greatest "bear" on Wall Street, Jesse Livermore, died a suicide; so did the president of the Bank of International Settlements.

If ever we are tempted to think that it is worth sacrificing morals and principles for the sake of money; if ever we are tempted to say, "If only I had wealth and freedom from financial worry, how happy I would be," we do well to meditate briefly on the statistics given above.

---

*Adapted.

> *For him (Christ) I have accepted the loss of everything, and I look on everything as so much rubbish, if only I can have Christ, and be given a place in him* (PHIL. 3, 8).

126   SECRETS OF YOUTH*

We seldom picture St. Francis of Assisi as an old man. Up to the very end of his life he maintained a youthful exuberance. He may not have said it, but he certainly lived the adage: age is not so much a physical condition as the climate of the soul.

He kept youthful and retained his buoyant outlook by reducing his wants to the simplest and the fewest. He resisted the tyranny of desire. He accepted whatever was given — the sun, rain, snow. No questioning. No fretting. No anxiety. He was satisfied to be cradled in the Eternal Arms.

It is only recently that psychologists have caught up with his formula. The recommendations they are giving us now sound like the rule and spirit Francis bequeathed to his followers:

Learn to like what does not cost much.

Learn to like reading, conversation, music.

Learn to like plain food, plain service.

Learn to like the song of birds, the companionship of animal, the laughter and gaiety of children.

Learn to like gardening, carpentry, puttering.

Learn to like the sunrise, the sunset, the beating of the rain on the roof, the gentle fall of snow.

Learn to keep your wants simple.

Learn to like work and enjoy the satisfaction of doing work well.

Learn to like people, no matter how different.

Air, light, sunshine, joy, happiness, people, life. These are the elements in the climate suggested by the psychologists. But don't they sound like something lifted from St. Francis' *Canticle of Brother Sun*?

This should be the climate of the soul at any stage of life. It is not a matter of passing years. It is a state of mind, the climate of the soul that determines one's age. So don't get old before your time.

Third Order Bulletin, Franciscan Herald Press, Chicago.

Let little children come to me; do not stop them; for it is to such as these that the kingdom of God belongs. I tell you solemnly, anyone who does not welcome the kingdom of God like a little child will never enter it (MK. 10, 14-15).

127   *LONG AND SHORT OF IT*

Jo Wan died and passed on to what the orientals envision as the next life. When he appeared before the judgment seat of God, he passed all the critical tests with flying colors and was sent to the oriental equivalent of heaven. He thanked God, but before he bowed out of the hallowed Presence, he made one strange request.

"May I visit hell?"

The request was granted and Jo Wan stood at the fiery gates of hell. The sights and sounds stirred him to his depths. There was the weeping and wailing and gnashing of teeth that he had heard about. There was something else that he had not heard about. Food lay all over the place in profuse abundance. Despite the evident great supply of food everybody was suffering the agonies of starvation. Jo Wan was puzzled. Each person held a set of chopsticks. There was plenty of food. Why the starvation?

As he observed the plight, Jo Wan noticed that each one was able to pick up the food with his chopsticks but was unable to get the food into his mouth because the chopsticks were too long. And the one unalterable rule of hell was that each person must hold the chopsticks on the very end. This was hell. Each one was completely centered on his own needs and was unable to satisfy them.

Jo Wan then went to heaven. There was the joy and glory and happiness that he had heard about. There was something more that he had not heard about. Here he found a strange similarity to the conditions that prevailed in hell. There was the same profuse abundance of food. Each person had the same pair of unusually long chopsticks. The exact unalterable rule was in effect — each one must hold the chopsticks at the very end which made it impossible for him to reach his own mouth.

But there was a big difference. Each person was feeding his neighbor and each in his turn was being fed by his neighbor. This was heaven. Each one was completely concerned about the needs of his neighbor. In this concern for his neighbor, his own needs were completely satisfied.

". . . . to love your neighbor as yourself, this is far more important than any holocaust or sacrifice. Jesus, seeing how wisely he had spoken, said, "You are not far from the kingdom of God."

If a man who was rich enough in this world's goods saw that one of his brothers was in need, but closed his heart to him, how could the love of God be living in him (1 Jn. 3, 17)?

128   DO IT NOW

A little "taffy" during life is worth more than all the "epitaphy" after death. Too little and too late is the anguished cry of so many of us. Often we think about the many things we could have done to make someone just a bit more happy, but now it is too late. Death intervened.

At the wake of her mother a little girl remarked, "Look at all those flowers. If only mother could have had some while she was alive. No one thought of giving her flowers and how she loved them. She used to walk through the floral shops just so she could smell their fragrance. But now it is too late."

If ever you are going to love me, love me now while I know
All the warm and tender feeling from real affection flow.
Love me while I am living. Don't wait till I am gone
And then chisel it on marble . . . warm love words on ice-stone.
If you have dear thoughts about me, why not whisper them
   to me?
Surely they would make me happy and as glad as glad can be.
If you wait till I am sleeping, never more to wake again
There'll be walls of earth between us and I cannot hear you
   then.
If you know someone were thirsting for a drink of water sweet
Would you then be slow in bringing it? Would you step with
   laggard feet?

There's a tender heart right near you that is thirsting for your
　　love.
Why should you refuse to give it, since God sent it from above?
You have flowers in your garden; some are white and some
　　are red.
Give them to me now while I am living. I can't see them when
　　I am dead.
I won't need your fond caresses when the grass grows over
　　my face,
I won't want your love and kisses in my last resting place.
So if you are ever going to love me, if for just a little bit
Won't you love me while I am living, so I can treasure it?

I don't know where this poem came from. I found it among
my collection. It expresses the message I want to convey. Perhaps
you will keep it for your collection.

Daughters of St. Paul

MASSACHUSETTS
50 St. Paul's Ave., Jamaica Plain, Boston, MA 02130 **617-522-8911.**
172 Tremont Street, Boston, MA 02111 **617-426-5464; 617-426-4230.**

NEW YORK
78 Fort Place, Staten Island, NY 10301 **718-447-5071; 718-447-5086.**
59 East 43rd Street, New York, NY 10017 **212-986-7580.**
625 East 187th Street, Bronx, NY 10458 **212-584-0440.**
525 Main Street, Buffalo, NY 14203 **716-847-6044.**

NEW JERSEY
Hudson Mall Route 440 and Communipaw Ave.,
Jersey City, NJ 07304 **201-433-7740.**

CONNECTICUT
202 Fairfield Ave., Bridgeport, CT 06604 **203-335-9913.**

OHIO
2105 Ontario Street (at Prospect Ave.), Cleveland, OH 44115 **216-621-9427.**
616 Walnut Street, Cincinnati, OH 45202 **513-421-5733**

PENNSYLVANIA
1719 Chestnut Street, Philadelphia, PA 19103 **215-568-2638; 215-864-0991.**

VIRGINIA
1025 King Street, Alexandria, VA 22314 **703-549-3806.**

SOUTH CAROLINA
243 King Street, Charleston, SC 29401 **803-577-0175.**

FLORIDA
2700 Biscayne Blvd., Miami, FL 33137 **305-573-1618.**

LOUISIANA
4403 Veterans Memorial Blvd. Metairie, LA 70006 **504-887-7631; 504-887-0113.**
423 Main Street, Baton Rouge, LA 70802 **504-343-4057; 504-381-9485.**

MISSOURI
1001 Pine Street (at North 10th), St. Louis, MO 63101 **314-621-0346.**

ILLINOIS
172 North Michigan Ave., Chicago, IL 60601 **312-346-4228; 312-346-3240.**

TEXAS
114 Main Plaza, San Antonio, TX 78205 **512-224-8101.**

CALIFORNIA
1570 Fifth Ave. (at Cedar Street), San Diego, CA 92101 **619-232-1442.**
46 Geary Street, San Francisco, CA 94108 **415-781-5180.**

WASHINGTON
2301 Second Ave., Seattle, WA 98121 **206-441-3300.**

HAWAII
1143 Bishop Street, Honolulu, HI 96813 **808-521-2731.**

ALASKA
750 West 5th Ave., Anchorage, AK 99501 **907-272-8183.**

CANADA
3022 Dufferin Street, Toronto 395, Ontario, Canada.